SELLING WITH SENSITIVITY

ACHIEVING SUCCESS IN DEATHCARE SALES
THROUGH EMPATHY, SERVICE, AND
CONNECTION

LIZA ALTENBURG

CONTENTS

For Dad.
I hope you're proud.

CHAPTER 1
INTRODUCTION

MORE THAN JUST A JOB

DEATH IS PERHAPS the most inevitable part of life, yet it remains one of the most challenging experiences of human existence. For those working in the deathcare industry, it can be tough to balance business with the need to show genuine care and kindness. Our job is to guide and help families during their most difficult times, offering both practical support and emotional comfort.

In this field, I've seen two very different types of professionals. Some show deep empathy and care, making a real positive difference. Sadly, some lack empathy and understanding. These individuals only contribute to the negative image of deathcare professionals, seen by some as taking advantage of people's pain for their own gain.

This book brings together my personal experiences of loss and healing, along with lessons I've learned in my career as a stereotype-fighting sales professional in multiple industries. I want to help fight the stigma and provide a useful guide for those wanting to make a positive difference while also achieving financial success.

In this book, we'll dive into the ins and outs of selling in the deathcare industry. Using my own experiences and insights, I'll provide practical advice to help you build the skills needed to support grieving families, all while achieving a solid income. My hope is that by sharing this, I can inspire a new generation of professionals who not only defy stereotypes but also understand the importance of showing real heart, care, and understanding in the sensitive world of deathcare.

But before we delve into the complexities of this profession, I want to invite you on a personal journey. It's a journey that changed my life and helped me understand the power of empathy and being true to yourself in the face of loss.

A MOMENT THAT CHANGED EVERYTHING

On the fateful afternoon of April 17, 2015, I received a call from my Uncle Reed. He had been trying to reach my dad to finalize their lunch plans, but without any response from him, he suggested I go check on him since I lived close by. Concerned, my 13-year-old son, Ryan, insisted on joining me, as he and his grandpa shared an incredibly close bond.

As we arrived at Dad's house, I sensed something was amiss. The closed blinds, unusual for that time of day, made me worry. I recalled a conversation I had with Dad a month prior, when he had jokingly mentioned that one day, I would be the one to find him dead in his home. At the time, we both laughed it off, never imagining it could become a reality so soon.

I asked Ryan to stay in the car while I went inside. The dimly lit interior and the barking of Dad's dog, Gracie, only heightened my anxiety. I searched the house, calling out for Dad, until I found him in his bedroom, slumped beside the bed. I touched him, desperately hoping the slight movement I saw was a sign of life.

As I rushed to call 911, I signaled to Ryan to stay put. In my panic, I found myself pleading with the dispatcher to hurry, just like in the movies. I called my then-girlfriend (now wife), Sarah, and my mom for support, as I still didn't know what was happening, and Ryan was waiting alone outside.

Paramedics arrived and assessed the situation, but I overheard one say, "He's cold." Ignoring the implications, I focused on the idea of Dad's potential hospital stay and need for a dog sitter. Mom arrived, and we waited anxiously together. The paramedics emerged and informed us that Dad had been gone for hours before they arrived. In shock, Mom and I comforted each other as we began to process the news.

Ryan's reaction was heart-wrenching - tears, denial, and more tears. Amid the chaos, I was grateful to have Sarah and Mom there to support Ryan and me. I called Uncle Reed to inform him of the tragedy and asked him to contact the rest of the family, and I was so grateful that he agreed.

As the medical examiner's office arrived to take Dad away, I couldn't bear to watch. I asked Sarah to keep Ryan occupied in the backyard with Gracie while I sat in the kitchen, listening to the sounds of my dad, my hero, being wheeled out of his house.

As the only child of my divorced father, I carried the weight of responsibility squarely on my shoulders. In my home state of Michigan, this meant that every decision had to be made by me, and every penny had to come out of my pocket. This immense responsibility created chaos beyond what should have been healthy grief, and it took nearly a year before I could even begin to emotionally process my loss.

In the days and weeks that followed Dad's death, I was confronted with the overwhelming task of making his final arrangements. It was during this difficult time that I came to understand the vital role of compassionate and empathetic deathcare professionals. The support and guidance they provided were instrumental in helping me navigate the complexities of loss and the many decisions that lay before me.

This deeply personal and transformative experience became the catalyst for my exploration of the deathcare industry and, ultimately, the driving force behind this book.

Selling with Sensitivity: Achieving Sales Success in Deathcare through Empathy, Service, and Connection is a culmination of my journey, a testament to the power of connection, empathy and authenticity, and a guide for deathcare professionals who serve families in their most vulnerable hours.

CHAPTER 2
BECOMING A COMPASSIONATE SALES PROFESSIONAL

OVER THE COURSE of my 20+ years in sales, I have had the opportunity to hone my skills, grow as a leader, and learn from my experiences. The lessons I learned have shaped my understanding of the importance of passion, ownership, and genuine connection in the world of sales.

These experiences have also taught me that the role of a salesperson goes far beyond simply closing deals and hitting targets. As deathcare sales professionals, we have the unique opportunity to help others transform their lives, achieve their goals, and create lasting memories for themselves and their families.

MY JOURNEY IN SALES AND ENTREPRENEURSHIP

My interest in sales and entrepreneurship took root early on, having grown up in a family business founded by my grandfather and his brother in the 1950s. My mom began working there at the age of 15 and, along with her two siblings, took over the business as the years went on. Even during his retirement, Grandpa would show up daily at the office, lending a hand wherever he could. His actions were a vivid display of undying passion and commitment. The powerful legacy he left behind was evident when he passed away in 2011, with a thriving small business that provided successful careers to three of his four children and three of his six grandchildren. I am inspired by the thought that this legacy may continue to offer livelihoods to future generations.

Witnessing Mom's leadership in our family business taught me the value of ownership. When challenges arose, she had no boss to blame and no supervisor to refer customers to - the buck truly stopped with her.

This powerful lesson has stayed with me; I will always consider Mom to be my first and most impactful business teacher. Throughout my formative years, I was able to witness her hiring, training, coaching, having difficult conversations, and generally prioritizing the professional and personal development of her staff members. It wasn't unusual to have a non-family employee at the holiday dinner table with our family. She always made sure that anyone she hired knew she valued them beyond their ability to generate revenue.

During my teen years, I worked alongside my family in the office. Despite the invaluable lessons and experiences gained during that time, I chose to explore a different path for my career. Mom's teachings about leadership and caring for others were deeply ingrained in me, and I knew that these lessons would guide me in whatever career path I pursued.

One of the most significant lessons Mom taught me was the importance of truly caring for the people I lead. This authentic approach to leadership would prove invaluable in my journey.

The entrepreneurial pull was strong within me, and I was determined to forge my own path. This drive led me to the world of sales and entrepreneurship, where I would build on the foundation laid by my family's business. As I began my career, I kept genuine care, responsibility, and empathy, instilled in me by Mom and Grandpa, at the heart of my approach.

At the beginning of my career, I took a leap of faith into the world of entrepreneurship, embarking on a journey in direct selling and network marketing. Working independently for my first seven years, I established a reputation for being a skilled and dedicated sales professional who genuinely cared about helping customers find the right solutions. I attended conferences, listened to books on tape (yes, tape - it was that long ago), and practiced all that I learned.

It was then that a seasoned industry expert with more than 30 years of experience saw something in me and offered me my first corporate role. Over the course of the six years that followed, this mentor took me under his wing, generously shared his wisdom, and encouraged my growth. I am forever grateful for his guidance and the opportunity he provided to the young, inexperienced 25-year-old me.

In the world of direct selling and network marketing, I learned the true value of hustle and problem-solving. Whether I was addressing beauty concerns, providing practical kitchenware, or offering organizational tools, I acted as a consultant and a problem solver. I knew who my ideal clients were, and I sold products that genuinely improved their lives. In doing so, I also built my first sales teams, mentoring and guiding them to achieve success in the same way that I had learned to do it. With Mom's lessons in leadership and authenticity at the heart of everything I did, I created a lucrative income for myself and helped others to do the same.

Two life-altering lessons emerged during my time in the corporate world of direct selling.

1. I came to understand how a negative industry stereotype can weigh heavily on a sales team. Stereotypes often have reality-based roots, much to the dismay of those adversely affected by them. In network marketing, the stereotype emerged from years of unregulated pyramid-style schemes, selfish, "me-focused" inward training that lacked an outward mindset or determination to truly help others, and the expectation that even the newest and most financially strapped sales representatives would purchase and carry stock they might never sell.

2. I realized that the only way to break free from this stigma was to disprove it day by day and interaction by interaction, by using and teaching tactics rooted in integrity, with a genuine focus on assisting others. This mission became my life's work.

Within the sphere of direct sales, I nurtured a passion for helping individual members of my sales team to dream big, establish bold goals, and apply prospecting and selling strategies to fulfill their ambitions.

One example that stands out is the story of a young mother, Monica, who came to me for help. Her goal was to take her family on a Disney vacation, but her husband dismissed the idea as too expensive and unrealistic. Monica was undeterred. Together, we devised a plan and scheduled regular accountability touch points. I trained and coached her as she pursued her business, which her husband condescendingly called her "little hobby." Seven months later, Monica achieved her goal by taking her family on the trip without any financial help from her husband. Her proudest moment was hearing him tell someone at the Disney Park that it was all thanks to her hard work and the income she earned running her business.

Tragically, less than a year later, Monica's teenage daughter was killed in a car accident. At the funeral, dozens of photos from that unforgettable Disney vacation were displayed.

Stories like Monica's have deeply fulfilled me and reinforced my belief in the power of sales to create lasting, meaningful impacts on people's lives. These experiences of personal achievement and triumph have fueled my passion throughout my career, inspiring me to continue helping others realize their dreams and make their own lasting memories.

TRANSITION INTO DEATHCARE SALES

My journey into the deathcare industry was fueled by my personal experience with loss and my newfound understanding of the vital role that compassionate professionals play in supporting families.

With a natural inclination toward and empathy and a knack for connecting with others, stepping into deathcare sales felt like a seamless transition for me. The approach of providing guidance and support, rooted in genuine care, resonated with me. It became clear that open conversations about death and advanced planning were essential, as I had witnessed firsthand the chaos and financial burden that can be avoided by addressing these matters in advance.

My own journey of loss taught me a valuable lesson: the power of open dialogue and proactive planning. If only we had overcome our hesitations and discussed his wishes surrounding his passing, I would have been spared the added heartache and financial stress. This realization ignited a fire within me to ensure that other families wouldn't have to endure a similar experience. Each interaction, every opportunity to guide families through an end-of-life journey, not only helped them but also facilitated my own healing process.

Stepping into the deathcare industry also meant confronting and dispelling the negative stereotypes that plague our field. Similar to the unwanted stigma associated with network marketing, the deathcare industry has had its share of unethical practices and broken promises. I embraced the opportunity to challenge these misconceptions head-on, the same way I had done so in network marketing - day by day and interaction by interaction.

As we embark on this journey together, remember that your role as a deathcare professional extends far beyond the transactions and numbers. By embodying empathy, compassion, and genuine heart-centered service (just like Mom taught me), I've aimed to build a legacy rooted in rewriting the narrative. Together, we can ignite a paradigm shift and create a more compassionate and dignified deathcare experience for all.

AN INTENTIONAL LACK OF DIFFERENTIATION

Navigating the delicate realm of grief and end-of-life planning requires a special touch and a true understanding of the emotional journey people undertake. Throughout this book, we'll explore various aspects of the deathcare industry, acknowledging that each client interaction is deeply personal and emotionally intense. You may have noticed that I chose not to split the book into separate sections for at-need client strategies (those who have experienced a loss and are working with you to arrange a funeral) and pre-need client strategies (those who are making end-of-life preparations in advance).

Why?

Well, whether someone is mourning the loss of a loved one or actively making end-of-life plans for themselves or another, they're bravely confronting mortality, and that brings forth a rollercoaster of emotions. By not compartmentalizing, we emphasize the interconnected nature of experiences and emotions that both at-need and pre-need clients undergo. The art of sensitive selling lies at the heart of our work, no matter who is sitting on the other side of the table.

In each client interaction, we must recognize the weight of their emotions and adapt our selling strategies accordingly. Sensitivity becomes the bedrock of our approach, creating a secure and supportive environment where individuals feel genuinely understood, heard, and respected. Throughout this book, we'll explore practical techniques and strategies that enable you to master the art of sensitive selling. From effective spoken and non-spoken communication to fostering a culture of empathy and service, you'll receive insights and practical advice to help you connect with clients in ways that honor and validate their unique emotional journeys.

As deathcare professionals, we have the privilege of supporting people as they navigate the complex web of life, loss, and legacy. By embracing the essence of sensitive selling, we respect the human experience and enable our clients to find solace, understanding, and comfort during life's most delicate moments.

So, as we begin this journey together, let's discover the power of sensitive selling. We'll unravel its importance, explore practical strategies, and traverse the intricacies of grief and advanced planning with warmth, empathy, and genuine care —regardless of whom we're serving at any given moment.

Get ready to make a difference, one heartfelt interaction at a time.

CHAPTER 3
PERCEPTION IS REALITY

WHILE YOUR INTENDED message might be fantastic in your mind, if it isn't perceived the way you intend by your clients, it's not going to hit home.

Regardless of how good your service is, how impressive you think a presentation is, or how hard you work to create a positive experience for someone, it all boils down to how it is received by your client. *Their* experiences, feelings, thoughts, and perceptions are the factors that determine the success of your interaction with them.

In this chapter, we'll strive to understand this intricate and fascinating aspect of human perception in sales. It's not always an easy task, but it's always worth the effort.

Empathy and sympathy might seem alike, but they're not quite the same.

Empathy is when you feel the same emotions as someone else, like you're in their shoes. It's all about understanding and sharing someone's feelings. Sympathy, though, is when you feel sad or sorry for someone else's tough time. It's not about sharing the feeling, but more about feeling bad for them. In simple words, empathy is feeling *with* people, and sympathy is feeling *for* them.

When you develop more empathy, you can adjust your behaviors to fit each family's emotional needs. Empathy can also help you to identify unspoken worries, giving you the opportunity to step in and deal with them before they become a bigger issue.

In every interaction with a client, keep this question in mind: "What if that was me?" Imagine you'd just lost the most important person in your life. Imagine having the bravery to confront your own mortality by sitting down with a total stranger and telling them details of your most guarded feelings about death and legacy. How would you want to be spoken to or treated? What would you need from the person who was guiding you?

To start actively practicing empathy, incorporate the following strategies into your interactions with families:

1. Avoid asking "how are you" as a greeting. Instead, opt for something more direct, like "Thank you for taking the time to come in today" or simply, "Hello."

———

During my early days in deathcare, while still in training, I was assigned a scavenger hunt on the cemetery grounds. I had a list of names of people laid to rest on-site, and my task was to locate and photograph their memorials. It was a gorgeous spring day, with clear blue skies and birds singing sweet melodies. Eager to complete my assignment, I grabbed the keys to the cemetery's golf cart and headed out.

As I made my way to the golf cart, I came across a man dressed casually in shorts and a t-shirt. Overflowing with cheerfulness, the default demeanor that I'd picked up selling fun products like lipstick and candles, I greeted him in a chipper tone, "How are you today?" The man nodded silently and continued along his path, and so did I, setting off to complete my task.

It wasn't until I returned to the office, over an hour later, that I discovered the true gravity of the situation. I found the man sobbing in the arms of my coworker, seeking comfort and support. He had been at the cemetery office to make final arrangements for his only child, a 17-year-old son, who had tragically died by suicide. Heartbreakingly, it was the father who had discovered his son's body in their home.

This experience taught me the importance of being mindful of my greetings, especially in the sensitive deathcare industry. We must always remember the emotional weight that families carry with them and adjust our approach accordingly.

———

2. When a death has occurred, offer sincere condolences to the grieving client, making eye contact and speaking softly. Being genuine is crucial, as inauthenticity can be easily detected and may leave families feeling like they are merely a means to an end.

––––––

Reflecting on my own experience as a newly bereaved daughter, I encountered both sincere and insincere condolences from deathcare professionals. The genuine compassion and care shown by the funeral director who offered heartfelt condolences are forever etched in my memory. In contrast, the insincere, words-only condolences given by his distracted colleague left a lasting impression of callousness that I am reminded of every time I see her, especially now that I work in the industry myself.

––––––

3. Ask open-ended questions that allow them to discuss their experience at their own pace, and listen actively, showing that you truly care.

4. Soften your vocabulary, using gentler terms like "urn" instead of "cremains" or "interment fee" instead of "opening and closing." This more delicate language can make a significant difference in the comfort of your client.

5. If you're not religious or you're unsure whether religious sentiments will be well-received, offer alternative expressions of support, such as "I'll be thinking of you and your family".

This inclusive approach ensures that everyone feels respected and cared for, regardless of their beliefs.

6. Keep the focus on the family's needs, not company policy or processes, or state or federal laws. Explain your processes in terms of how they affect and benefit the family, not just because they're required.

You play a vital role in guiding families through one of the most challenging times of their lives.

Remember to be patient with yourself as you develop your empathetic skills. As you gain experience and learn from the stories of others, you'll become more adept at providing compassionate, empathetic support.

READING AND RESPONDING TO EMOTIONAL CUES

Emotional cues can be verbal or nonverbal and may vary in intensity and complexity. By paying close attention to these cues, you can gain insights into the emotional state of your client and tailor your approach accordingly. Following are some strategies for reading and responding to emotional cues, along with appropriate responses for each.

Observe body language. Nonverbal cues, such as facial expressions, posture, and gestures, can reveal a person's emotional state. Look for signs of tension, sadness, or anger in their body language, and adjust your approach accordingly.

Appropriate response: If you notice a grieving person clenching their fists or tightening their jaw, acknowledge the tension and encourage them to take a few deep breaths or even step out for a little bit of fresh air.

Listen for tone and pitch. The tone and pitch of a person's voice can convey emotions that may not be apparent in their words. Pay attention to any changes in the volume, pitch, or tone, as these can indicate emotional shifts or underlying feelings.

Appropriate Response: If the person's voice becomes shaky or breaks, offer a comforting touch or a tissue, assure them that you're not in a hurry, and give them space to regain their composure before continuing the conversation.

Pay attention to word choice. The words people choose to express their emotions can provide insights into their emotional state. Be aware of any recurring themes or phrases that may indicate unresolved feelings or emotional pain.

Appropriate Response: If a grieving person repeatedly mentions feeling guilty, gently explore the reasons behind their guilt and reassure them that this is a common emotion during the grieving process.

Validate and acknowledge emotions. When you recognize an emotional cue, validate the person's feelings by acknowledging their feelings and expressing empathy. This can help create a safe space for them to share their thoughts and emotions openly.

Appropriate response: If the person shares feeling hopeless and unable to see a future without their loved one, say something like, "It's completely understandable that's the way you feel right now. For now, let's just take things one minute at a time."

Ask open-ended questions. Encourage your client to share their feelings and experiences by asking open-ended questions. This can help them explore their emotions more deeply and provide you with valuable insights into their emotional state.

Appropriate response: Ask questions like, "Had he/she been sick for long?" In my personal experience, asking this question just after offering condolences allows the family to tell you the story of their loved one's death if it would be cathartic for them. If they don't feel the pull to share, they'll shut you down with a one-word "yes" or "no," and you'll know they're not in a chatty mood and need you to simply guide them through the process they're relying on you for.

Be present and attentive. By maintaining eye contact and offering supportive gestures, such as nodding or leaning in, you can show the grieving person that you are genuinely interested in their emotions and willing to listen.

Appropriate response: If the person seems hesitant to share their feelings, reassure them by saying, "I'd love to hear more about your loved one." Replace "loved one" with "mom," "dad," "or friend," as appropriate.

Offer appropriate support. Based on the emotional cues you have identified, offer support that is tailored to the individual's needs. This may involve providing a listening ear, sharing comforting words, or offering practical assistance.

Appropriate response: If your client's cues signal overwhelm, reassure them that you are going to handle the bulk of the work during their experience with your funeral home or cemetery. Understanding that they can truly rely on you can help them to feel that you've taken something significant off their already-full plate and allow them to focus on the things that truly need their attention.

By developing the ability to read and respond to common emotional cues in the bereaved, you can create a supportive environment for grieving individuals and help them navigate the complex emotions that accompany loss.

CULTIVATING SELF-AWARENESS

Understanding your own emotions, strengths, and weaknesses can help you interact effectively with the clients you serve. A popular tool for increasing self-awareness is the Myers-Briggs Type Indicator (MBTI) personality test. The MBTI assesses personality preferences across four spectrums:

1. **Extroversion-Introversion:** Do you direct your energy inward or outward?

2. **Sensing-Intuition:** How do you receive and absorb information?

3. Thinking-Feeling: How do you make decisions?

4. Judging-Perceiving: How do you process the world around you?

A free, simplified version of the MBTI test, available at 16personalities.com, can provide you with personalized insights into your own style. By taking this test, you can gain a better understanding of your tendencies and preferences, which can help you recognize your strengths and areas for growth when it comes to handling the clients you serve.

As you explore the MBTI and delve into the different personality types, you may discover that you resonate with aspects of multiple types. It's important to keep in mind that the MBTI is a spectrum, and human personalities are wonderfully complex and multifaceted.

For instance, personally, I generally align with the characteristics of INFJ (Introversion-Intuition-Feeling-Judging), but there are days when I find myself leaning more toward Extroversion than Introversion. This shift is often influenced by my current level of outgoingness and the energy I feel within. While I tend to value quiet recharging time, it doesn't mean I don't enjoy being in the company of others.

By embracing the fluidity of our personalities and recognizing that we can exhibit traits from different types, we gain a more holistic understanding of ourselves and how we interact with others. It's perfectly normal to see variations within ourselves across the MBTI spectrum, as it reflects the intricate nature of humanity.

So, as you explore the MBTI and find pieces of yourself across the spectrum, know that it's entirely normal and part of the beautiful tapestry that makes you unique. Embrace the nuances and complexities of your personality, and use the insights from the MBTI as a valuable tool for self-discovery and personal growth.

Once you have taken the test and identified your personality type, review the following tables that identify a couple of strengths and opportunities for growth associated with each trait. This will help you develop a personalized approach to interacting with your clients while improving your emotional intelligence.

EXTROVERSION-INTROVERSION

Extroversion (E)	Introversion (I)
Strengths:	Strengths:
• Easily engages with grieving families. • Provides emotional support through open communication. • Easily engages in conversations and establishes rapport. • Expresses warmth and empathy verbally.	• Good at active listening and providing a calm presence. • Respects the need for personal space and quiet moments. • Naturally inclined to listen more than speak. • Provides a calming and supportive presence.
Opportunities for Growth:	Opportunities for Growth:
• Practice active listening and avoid dominating conversations. • Respect the need for personal space and quiet moments. • Focus on active listening and resist the urge to interrupt or dominate the conversation. • Be mindful of nonverbal cues and the emotional atmosphere.	• Push yourself to initiate conversations and express empathy verbally. • Develop strategies to manage energy levels during emotionally intense interactions. • Work on verbally expressing empathy and support. • Develop strategies for maintaining energy levels during emotionally intense.

SENSING-INTUITION

Sensing (S)	Intuition (N)
Strengths:	Strengths:
• Attentive to practical and specific needs and details shared by clients. • Provides concrete assistance and support. • Grounded in the present reality and experiences.	• Skilled at understanding the emotional and abstracts of grief. • Open to exploring different coping strategies and perspectives. • Able to connect the dots and understand underlying patterns.
Opportunities for Growth:	Opportunities for Growth:
• Develop the ability to recognize and address emotional and abstract aspects of grief. • Be open to exploring different coping strategies and perspectives. • Learn to read between the lines and understand implicit messages.	• Pay more attention to practical details and immediate needs. • Ensure that support and assistance are grounded in present reality. • Stay focused on the present moment and the individual's immediate needs.

THINKING-FEELING

Thinking (T)	Feeling (F)
Strengths:	Strengths:
• Capable of maintaining objectivity and clear thinking, even during emotionally charged conversations. • Provides practical solutions and advice. • Analyzes and comprehends issues and emotional complexities.	• Naturally empathetic and emotionally attuned to others. • Creates strong emotional connections with clients. • Validates and supports the emotional experiences of others.
Opportunities for Growth:	Opportunities for Growth:
• Develop the ability to express empathy and emotional support. • Embrace the importance of emotional connection in the grieving process. • Focus on validating the emotional aspects of the client experience.	• Develop the ability to maintain objectivity and set boundaries. • Balance emotional support with practical solutions and advice. • Redirect the conversation from an emotional tangent back to the task at hand.

JUDGING-PERCEIVING

Judging (J)	Perceiving (P)
Strengths:	Strengths:
• Organized and efficient in providing support and resources. • Provides structure and stability in conversations, redirecting as needed. • Helps others to set goals and find a sense of direction.	• Adaptable and open-minded, flexible in response to the changing needs of others. • Open to exploring different approaches and coping strategies. • Encourages others to explore their emotions freely.
Opportunities for Growth:	Opportunities for Growth:
• Be flexible and patient, adapting to the changing needs of others. • Be open to exploring different approaches and coping strategies. • Allow the conversation to unfold naturally without trying to control the outcome.	• Develop organizational skills and provide structure for clients. • Balance adaptability with the need for stability and consistency. • Be mindful of time constraints and other practical considerations.

Please note that this is a simplified analysis, and individual strengths and opportunities may vary based on unique personality profiles. Taking the test at 16personalities.com and reflecting on your results can help you become more self-aware and better equipped to support your clients with empathy and understanding.

Building self-awareness is a key part in growing empathy and emotional intelligence. It helps you understand your own feelings, strengths, and weaknesses. With this knowledge, you can interact more effectively with clients. Tools like the Myers-Briggs Type Indicator (MBTI) personality test can help you see your strengths, as well as the areas where you can improve. By taking the time to think about your personality traits and how they affect your interactions, you can make a tailored approach that fits the unique needs of the families you serve.

For a personalized guide that can help you to translate your MBTI type into your sales career, visit sellingwithsensitivity.com/bonuses.

CHAPTER 4
THE CORE PRINCIPLES OF SELLING WITH SENSITIVITY

WITH A SOLID BASE IN SELF-AWARENESS, you'll be better equipped to embody the four main principles of selling with sensitivity: authenticity, emotional intelligence, integrity, and compassionate communication. In this chapter, we'll look at each of these principles in more detail. We'll review helpful strategies and advice on how to use them in your sales process. By mastering these skills, you'll improve your professional reputation and make a lasting impact on the lives of those you serve. This will show your commitment to providing top-notch care and support when they need it most.

AUTHENTICITY

You have likely been provided with various training materials and resources - perhaps by your company, perhaps through other means. These resources probably include call scripts, presentation decks, and flowcharts. While these tools can be incredibly valuable in guiding your sales process, it's important to understand that they will leave you with lackluster results if you don't come across as genuine and authentic when using them. Reading scripts as written may not accurately represent your personality and communication style, which can create a disconnect with your clients.

To make the most of these company-provided training materials and resources while maintaining authenticity, consider the following:

1. Understand the Purpose. Familiarize yourself with the purpose behind the training materials and resources provided. This will help you gain a clear understanding of the objectives they aim to achieve, allowing you to adapt them to your unique style while still meeting those goals.

2. Analyze and Adapt, Finding Your Own Voice: Reflect on your communication style and identify the unique qualities you can bring to the sales process. Analyze the training materials and resources to determine which key points and phrases most resonate with you. Use this knowledge to adapt the resources to better align with your natural communication style without reinventing the wheel. By making the resources your own, you can create a more authentic connection with clients.

———

As a new sales professional at a cemetery, I was inspired by my trainer's smooth delivery when role-playing the appointment-setting phone call script. Her ability to handle objections and keep the conversation flowing seamlessly left me eager to try it out myself.

However, after being given a call list later that week, I found myself hearing "no" after "no" on my calls, despite using the same script as my trainer. Frustrated and on my sixty-somethingth call of the day, I spotted a squirrel struggling to climb up the building gutter outside. Mesmerized, I found myself watching the furry little creature while I spoke to my next prospect. That mindless act left me unable to read the script in front of me, and I unintentionally strayed from it, using my own words instead. To my surprise, it worked. I booked an appointment – and happy-danced in my chair.

This experience taught me the power of using my own voice and authentic communication style when connecting with prospects and clients. After logging my first successful appointment, I took the initiative to rewrite the script in my own words, resulting in a significant increase in my appointment-setting rate.

Months later, I discovered that my trainer's success with the script was due to her having written it herself. No wonder she'd been so successful with it – it was totally authentic to her! I realized that by using her words, I wasn't coming across as genuine. This experience taught me the importance of finding my own voice and using it to connect with prospects and clients in a meaningful way.

———

3. Practice, Practice, Practice: To ensure that your revised training materials and resources flow naturally, practice using them in various scenarios. This can help you become more comfortable and confident in your delivery, allowing you to connect with prospective clients more effectively.

4. Seek Feedback: Share your adapted training materials and resources with a trusted colleague or mentor, and ask for their feedback. Their insights can help you refine your approach and further enhance your authenticity.

5. Stay Flexible: Remember that no training material or resource can account for every possible situation or interaction. Be prepared to deviate from your adapted resources when necessary to address the unique needs and concerns of each client. Staying flexible and responsive to individual circumstances will demonstrate your commitment to providing compassionate and personalized care.

By using your resources in your own way and adding your unique voice, you can form a genuine bond with your clients. This method helps build trust and makes the experience better for clients during what may be an incredibly challenging time. As you continue to hone your authenticity and adapt your resources, you'll become a more empathetic and effective sales professional.

INTEGRITY

Integrity is the foundation of any strong professional relationship, especially in the deathcare industry, where clients are often vulnerable and seeking guidance during difficult times. I've heard integrity well-defined as "doing the right thing, even when no one's looking." Exhibiting integrity involves putting the needs and best interests of your clients first and offering genuine support and guidance without any ulterior motives or unethical practices.

$\bullet \quad \bullet \quad \bullet$

To practice integrity in deathcare sales, be conscious of the following:

1. **Be truthful:** Always provide accurate and honest information to your clients. Avoid exaggerating or misrepresenting your products or services, as this can erode trust and damage your credibility.

2. **Be transparent:** Clearly communicate your intentions and the reasoning behind your recommendations. This openness will help clients feel more comfortable and confident in their decision-making process.

3. **Act ethically:** Follow industry best practices and adhere to any applicable laws and regulations. This includes respecting client confidentiality and privacy, as well as honoring any cultural or religious preferences your client may have.

4. **Prioritize client needs:** Focus on understanding and addressing the unique needs of each client rather than pushing for a sale or promoting a specific product or service. Offer solutions that genuinely meet their preferences, and be prepared to adjust your approach based on their individual circumstances.

5. **Maintain accountability:** If you make a mistake or a misunderstanding occurs, take responsibility, and work towards resolving the issue promptly and professionally.

Demonstrating accountability fosters trust and reinforces your commitment to ethical behavior.

6. Make good on your word: Follow through on your commitments and communicate with clients as promised. If you tell a family that they'll hear from you by a certain time, make sure they do, even if you don't have an answer or solution for them yet. Don't leave them guessing or wondering whether you forgot about them. In this way, you demonstrate that they are valued and important to you.

By practicing integrity, you strengthen your professional reputation and foster trust and credibility with your clients. They will feel reassured that they are being guided by a compassionate and ethical professional who genuinely cares about their well-being. Upholding integrity as a core principle of selling with sensitivity ultimately leads to better client relationships, improved customer satisfaction, and long-term business success.

EMOTIONAL INTELLIGENCE

Emotional intelligence (EI) encompasses the ability to identify, comprehend, and regulate your emotions, as well as the emotions of those around you. This skill allows you to effectively navigate intricate social situations and respond to the emotional needs of your clients.

By honing your EI, you can better anticipate and address clients' concerns, making it more feasible to identify solutions tailored to their specific needs.

EI allows you to navigate two key aspects of the sales process: understanding and managing your own emotions, and accurately perceiving and responding to the emotional needs of the clients you serve. When combined with empathy, emotional intelligence forms a potent tool for fostering meaningful connections and delivering an exceptional level of support.

The first aspect that EI empowers you to master is your own emotional state. It encourages you to be aware of and address your emotions proactively, ensuring that you enter each interaction with emotional readiness.

By acknowledging and addressing your own emotions beforehand, whether it's taking a moment for self-reflection, practicing self-care, or seeking support from colleagues or mentors, you can ensure that you are fully present and emotionally available to meet the needs of the families you serve.

––––––

When my son Ryan was fifteen years old, I found myself in the midst of an incredibly challenging week as a parent. Emotions ran high at home, and every interaction seemed to be filled with tension and turmoil (parents of teenagers - sound familiar?). It was precisely during this tumultuous time that I received a heart-wrenching call at work, from a couple who had tragically lost their own fifteen-year-old son.

As I listened to their devastating story, my intuition sent a clear message: I wasn't emotionally equipped to handle the weight of this particular burial. However, my determination to prove myself as a capable professional, someone who could handle any situation, clouded my judgment. I neglected to prioritize my own emotional well-being, and as a consequence, I found myself guiding this shattered couple through the painful process of burying their teenage son.

The heaviness of my personal struggles made it increasingly difficult to provide the level of care and support that the grieving family deserved. I had to dig deep and summon every ounce of strength within me to navigate the complexities of the situation. I tried to compartmentalize the chaos of my own parenting struggles at home and consciously ignore the undeniable similarities between my own son and the son they had lost.

In hindsight, I recognize that there was support available to me during that challenging time. A simple conversation with my boss or a coworker would have led to a reassignment, or at the very least, additional resources, allowing me to prioritize my own well-being while ensuring that this particular family received the care of a counselor who was truly prepared for the task. It was a humbling experience that served as a stark reminder of the importance of recognizing my own limitations and the value of seeking support when it's needed most.

———

EI also enables you to discern and respond to the emotional cues and needs of the families you encounter. Each family's experience through an end-of-life journey is unique, and it is your role to adapt your approach accordingly. There are no cookie-cutter interactions in deathcare sales.

Your EI guides you in moments when you instinctively offer a tissue to a client as you notice their eyes welling with tears. It's the intuitive nudge that tells you to provide space for a family to discuss their options privately, respecting their need for reflection. EI is the gentle reminder in your mind that prompts you to offer a bottle of water and a snack to someone who has just experienced one of the most challenging days of their life in your office.

It's through these small acts of empathy and awareness that EI manifests itself in your interactions with clients. Offering a tissue acknowledges their pain and provides a simple gesture of comfort. Allowing families the space they need demonstrates respect for their privacy and allows them to process through their thoughts and emotions. Providing refreshments acknowledges the toll that emotional experiences can take on individuals, offering a small measure of care and physical nourishment.

These seemingly insignificant actions can make a significant impact on the emotional well-being of those you serve. They demonstrate your attentiveness, empathy, and commitment to providing holistic support during difficult times.

By attuning yourself to your client's emotional state, you can determine when to provide space for them to process their thoughts and emotions, when to slow down to ensure comprehension and ease any concerns, and when to offer repetition or clarification to address their specific needs. Additionally EI allows you to intuitively recognize the appropriate moments to pause for questions, provide reassurance, step out to allow a family time to discuss, or simply offer a compassionate presence.

In essence emotional intelligence serves as a guiding compass throughout the sales process. By mastering your own emotions and understanding those of your clients, you can build strong connections, navigate challenges with empathy, and provide the support and care that families facing end-of-life arrangements truly deserve.

Developing your emotional intelligence is essential for selling with sensitivity, allowing you to connect deeply with clients and provide the compassionate care they need when confronting their mortality. Professionals who exhibit EI are often more successful in their careers, as they can adeptly manage relationships and adapt to various situations.

COMPASSIONATE COMMUNICATION

Compassionate communication lies at the heart of the death-care profession, as it allows us to connect deeply with individuals and families during their most vulnerable moments. It is a powerful tool that encompasses both verbal and nonverbal aspects, enabling us to convey empathy, understanding, and support. By incorporating emotional intelligence into our approach, we enhance our ability to engage in compassionate communication. In the following sections, we will explore the importance of both verbal and nonverbal communication, delving into techniques that can foster meaningful connections and facilitate healing throughout the end-of-life journey.

Effective Verbal Communication

The way we speak, the words we choose, and the tone we convey can make a profound impact on the client experience. In this section, we explore key strategies for fostering compassionate communication that allows our clients to feel seen, heard, and supported. Let's explore the essential practices of effective verbal communication.

1. Be mindful of your tone and pace. In sensitive situations like dealing with grieving individuals or guiding a client through confronting their own mortality, the tone and pace of your speech play a vital role in conveying compassion and understanding. Speak softly and calmly and allow space for your client to process your words and respond in their own time.

Having spent over 20 years in high-energy sales environments, where enthusiasm and quick-paced communication were the norm, the transition to the deathcare industry was a bit of a culture shock for me.

In my previous sales roles, I had been trained to fill every moment of silence, considering it a sign of weakness or a missed opportunity.

"Dead air," as it was called, was something I instinctively tried to avoid. I quickly realized that this approach didn't align with the sensitive nature of deathcare sales.

One particular concept that challenged my ingrained habits was the importance of leaving space for clients to process information. I had to learn that silence wasn't something to fear or rush to fill, but rather a valuable tool for allowing clients to absorb and reflect on the information they've received.

During client interactions, I would find myself pausing after providing important details or discussing sensitive topics. The silence that followed was uncomfortable at first, and my initial instinct was to break it with more words. However, I gradually recognized the power of allowing information to hang in the air, giving clients the necessary time to process at their own pace.

I discovered that by embracing the concept of "dead air" and allowing moments of silence, I created an environment where clients felt heard and respected. It gave them space to ask questions, share their thoughts, and express their emotions without feeling rushed, overwhelmed, or pressured. This intentional pause became a powerful tool in building trust and establishing a compassionate connection with my clients.

Reflecting on client surveys completed after I assisted them with laying a loved one to rest or facilitating their end-of-life plans (come on, we all keep those surveys, don't we? No? Just me?), one adjective consistently stood out in my client's descriptions of me as a service-provider: "patient". I attribute that perception to my delib-

erate efforts in slowing down and embracing the power of "dead air."

---

2. Use empathetic language: Choose words that express empathy and understanding rather than trying to offer solutions or advice. Phrases such as "What you're carrying is very heavy," "this is very difficult, take your time," or "I'm here to support you" can help the person feel seen and heard during a sensitive time.

3. Validate the person's feelings: When a potential client shares their emotions, validate and acknowledge their feelings by saying something like, "It's completely normal to feel this way" or "I can understand why you would feel that way." This can help the person feel more comfortable and open in sharing their emotions.

4. Listen actively: Practice active listening by giving the person your full attention, maintaining eye contact, and offering supportive gestures such as nodding or leaning in. Resist the urge to interrupt, interject, check your phone, or let your eyes move to the clock; and allow the person to express their thoughts and feelings completely before you respond.

5. Be genuine and sincere: As you communicate, ensure that your words and actions are genuine and sincere. Avoid clichés or platitudes that may come across as insincere or dismissive of the person's feelings. Instead, speak from the heart and be honest in your expressions of empathy and support.

6. When grief is involved, avoid communicating a silver lining: Even if you mean well, avoid offering platitudes or trying to find a silver lining when someone is grieving. Saying things like "Everything happens for a reason," "They're in a better place," or "God never gives us more than we can handle," can seem uncaring and dismissive of the person's emotions. Instead, just be there for them, listen, and give support.

By focusing on effective verbal communication, you can create a compassionate and supportive environment for your clients to feel heard, understood, and comforted as they navigate their journey.

The Power of Nonverbal Communication

Our actions, not just our words, carry great weight in showing care, understanding, and support to people who are grieving or facing their own mortality. By being aware of our own nonverbal signals, we can make sure that our presence and actions are received as the service we intend, rather than as a sales pitch. Let's explore the essential practices of nonverbal communication.

1. Maintain eye contact: Establishing and maintaining eye contact while speaking to a potential client demonstrates your attentiveness and care. It helps create a connection and fosters a sense of trust between you and the individual.

2. Be mindful of your facial expressions: Ensure that your facial expressions convey understanding and openness. A soft, relaxed expression can help put your potential client at ease and make them feel more comfortable sharing their emotions with you.

3. Use appropriate body language: Adopt an open and inviting posture, such as facing the person directly, uncrossing your arms, and leaning slightly forward. In this way, you communicate your willingness to engage, serve, and support.

4. Offer comforting gestures: Small gestures like a gentle touch on the arm or shoulder, holding the person's hand, or offering a hug can provide comfort and reassurance when words may not be enough. Always be mindful of the individual's personal boundaries and cultural differences, and seek permission. A simple question like "May I give you a hug?" is the perfect way to ensure that your gestures are welcome and helpful

5. Pay attention to personal space: Respect your client's personal space and adjust your distance accordingly. Some individuals may appreciate physical closeness during difficult moments, while others may require more space to feel comfortable.

6. Mirror the person's body language: Subtly mirroring the person's body language, such as matching their pace of speech or adopting a similar posture, can help create a sense of rapport and understanding, making them feel more at ease in opening up.

7. Be aware of your own emotional cues: As a deathcare professional, you must manage your own emotions and maintain composure in difficult situations. Be mindful of any signs that you might be projecting your own feelings, such as nervousness, anxiety, or sadness, and focus on maintaining a calm and empathetic presence.

Harnessing the power of nonverbal communication enables you to create a supportive and compassionate environment. It allows your clients to express their emotions and feel understood and comforted as they navigate the journey through which you're guiding them.

CHAPTER 5
DEATHCARE SALES PRINCIPLES

EMOTIONAL COMPLEXITY

WELCOME to the world of deathcare sales, where emotions run high, and sensitivity is key. This is not your typical sales job. Unlike selling cars or gadgets, you're dealing with people at their most vulnerable. They're confused and probably overwhelmed by the numerous decisions they need to make. In the midst of this emotional whirlwind, your role is to provide guidance, support, and a sense of calm, all while keeping your sales objectives in mind.

The emotional complexity of deathcare sales can be both a challenge and an opportunity. To help you navigate this unique environment, let's explore five concepts to implement into your daily sales focus:

1. Empathetic, Authentic Connection: Begin by genuinely connecting with the families you serve. Actively listen to their stories, understand their needs, and acknowledge their pain.

This connection earns their trust and provides valuable insights to tailor your sales approach to their specific needs. Recognizing and validating their emotions will display empathy and build trust and rapport. Leading with connection will create a comfortable environment for open and honest communication, showing your focus on providing support and guidance rather than just making a sale. As a deathcare professional, you carry the heavy responsibility of helping families honor and celebrate their loved ones. Approach this responsibility with care and professionalism, remembering that you're providing a meaningful, lasting experience. Patience, empathy, and understanding are crucial as you navigate the wide range of emotions families experience during this difficult time.

2. Solution-Based Selling and Realistic Expectations: Focus on offering tailored solutions that genuinely benefit the family rather than pushing for a sale. Identify their needs and provide recommendations that demonstrate your genuine desire to help, creating a win-win situation. Be transparent and honest about the products and services you offer. Set realistic expectations to avoid misunderstandings and ensure the family feels well-informed and confident in their decision. Clear and concise communication is essential… Remember, you'll often be dealing with clients who are maneuvering through the fog of grief – make no assumptions that simple explanations will suffice.

––––––

Early in my tenure as a sales manager, I had an experience that underscored the significance of clear communication and managing expectations. During a pre-burial meeting at the cemetery, Anna, a diligent and eager cemetery counselor, discussed the process of a niche-side inurnment with a family. She explained that their service could last up to 30 minutes, and immediately afterward, the cemetery staff would place and seal the urn into its niche.

However, a few days later, the family arrived for their scheduled service and was disappointed to learn that the cemetery hadn't provided a pastor or ceremony leader for their memorial. They believed that Anna had conveyed the duration of the cemetery-organized service rather than providing guidance for their own planning and organization.

Although Anna had not intentionally misled them, their interpretation differed from her intention, and the client's perception was reality. This story serves as a powerful reminder of the importance of clear communication and managing expectations to avoid misunderstandings and ensure a positive experience for everyone involved.

———

3. Mindful Persistence and Self-Reflection: Be empathetic and understanding while staying mindful of your sales goals. Focus on prospecting for new advanced planning families, gently follow up with previous contacts, and ensure that all families feel your sincere care and support. Regularly assess your sales performance, including evaluating your balance of emotional intelligence and sales goals. Seek feedback from families, colleagues, and mentors to identify areas for improvement and growth, recognizing that personal development is an ongoing process with room for continuous improvement.

4. Belief in Your Products and Services: Believing in the value of advanced planning yourself is crucial for effectively communicating its benefits to your clients. When you genuinely understand and appreciate the advantages of end-of-life planning, you can confidently and passionately convey its significance in providing peace of mind, easing the emotional and financial burden on loved ones, and ensuring that a person's final wishes are honored.

────

My personal belief in the power of what I do as an advanced planning professional rises and falls on this unequivocal fact: One day, my son Ryan will face the responsibility of making my end-of-life arrangements. As my final act of parenting, I can choose now how that process will unfold for him.

Will he enter the arrangement room wide-eyed and uncertain, burdened with countless unasked questions - like how I entered the room when I lost my dad? Or will he arrive with my predetermined wishes in hand, his sole duty on that difficult day being to sign a few papers, knowing that I made all necessary arrangements years prior, leaving him with no decisions to make or costs to bear?

────

The belief that what you offer is truly beneficial to those you serve not only strengthens the trust and rapport you build with clients; it also enhances your ability to empathize with their concerns, address objections, and ultimately guide them towards making informed decisions that will positively impact their families for years to come. Take some time for internal reflection here... Why do you believe in the products or services you provide? Get clear on this, and let it drive every sales conversation you have moving forward.

5. Uncovering Opportunities Amidst Challenges: The emotional complexity of deathcare sales may seem daunting at first, but it also presents a unique opportunity for growth and personal fulfillment. Your role in deathcare sales is an opportunity to create deep connections and be a beacon of light during a difficult time.

By balancing emotional intelligence and sales goals, you'll not only excel in your deathcare sales career but also make a profound impact on the lives of the families you serve. Embrace the challenge and remember that your ability to connect with people on an emotional level is your greatest asset in this unique sales environment.

SERVICE OVER SALES

Visualize with me for a moment, the word "sales" in all caps.

S A L E S

What comes to mind? Perhaps aggressive salespeople, pushy tactics, and a relentless focus on closing deals, regardless of the customer's needs, abilities, or emotions. In many industries, this stereotype is unfortunately all too common, and it's crucial to break free from these preconceptions and embrace a different approach.

Now, as you continue to visualize, imagine a big shoe coming down and stepping on the word SALES, crushing it totally. As it lifts, a new word becomes visible.

S E R V I C E

This change symbolizes a vital shift in thinking that's necessary for success in sales, especially in situations requiring sensitivity. By putting service before sales, you make the experience better for your clients and build a lasting and fulfilling career for yourself.

While working in the cosmetics industry, I once met with Mary, a sales representative who had been selling cosmetics for more than 15 years. She was consistently achieving about 50% of the sales necessary to be recognized in the company's President's Club – the prestigious top seller's designation. When we met to discuss her business, I challenged her to double her sales by shifting her focus from selling her favorite product (lipstick) to solving her clients' problems. By asking questions, listening to their concerns, and recommending appropriate solutions, Mary tripled her sales in the next year and was even recognized as a most improved top seller within the company.

If this result can be accomplished by selling lipstick and face cream, just imagine what the service-over-sales strategy can do for you in deathcare.

The focus should always be on providing genuine, compassionate service to the families with whom you work. This means listening to their needs, understanding their emotions, and guiding them through the difficult process of end-of-life planning. Instead of pushing for a sale, aim to build trust and rapport by fostering an environment in which clients feel comfortable discussing their concerns and exploring their options.

To truly embrace a service-over-sales mindset in deathcare sales, consider the following principles:

Consciously Exercise Your Authenticity.

Approach each interaction with honesty and sincerity. Be genuine in your desire to help families, and let that authenticity guide your actions.

- *While Mary was certainly authentic when her sales focus was on lipstick (because it was her favorite product), once she expanded her knowledge about her product base and even started to use some of the other products herself, she was able to have authentic conversations about her recommendations based on her clients' needs.*

How familiar are you with all of the products and services that you offer? Be sure that you're not limiting yourself by staying in your comfort zone while presenting options to families.

Listen Deeply.

Active listening is important in any sales, particularly in deathcare sales. Give families the space to express their thoughts, emotions, and concerns. Show that you truly care about what they have to say and that you are there to support them.

- *Mary's new approach involved asking her clients about their aesthetic problems and listening carefully to their responses, which enabled her to provide tailored solutions that addressed their specific needs.*

There's nothing to sell until you know your clients' needs and wants. The beginning of any interaction should be full of conversational questions that help you to determine what options should be presented during your time together.

Educate and Inform.

Your role as a deathcare sales professional is to provide valuable information and guidance. Share your knowledge and expertise with families to help them make informed decisions that align with their needs and values.

- *As Mary broadened her understanding of the product line and its ingredients, she became a more effective educator, better able to guide her clients to choose the products that would truly benefit them based on their concerns and preferences. The sales process became easier for her as she began to sell the products that her clients truly needed, rather than the ones they were willing to try only after she sold them on her passion for it.*

Use your emotional intelligence to educate your families. For example, if cost is prohibiting your client from considering an option you feel could be right for them, take the opportunity to educate them on the financial options that could make a more expensive option doable for them.

Focus on building relationships.

Develop long-lasting relationships with the families you work with by being consistently present, supportive, and reliable. You've likely heard the term "under-promise and over-deliver"—this is a perfect place to implement it. Keep promises that you make, follow up sooner than your clients expect, and ensure that every interaction leaves your clients feeling heard and supported.

- *As Mary shifted her focus to solving her clients' problems and addressing their concerns, she naturally built stronger relationships with them. These connections not only led to increased sales but also to a more rewarding and fulfilling experience for both Mary and her clients.*

Your clients should not be archived once they've purchased from you. Continuing to provide your families with service and care will deepen your connections and open opportunities for profound healing, lasting relationships, and positive word-of-mouth referrals within your community.

By prioritizing service over sales, you can create a meaningful, fulfilling career in deathcare sales. Your compassionate approach will resonate with families, helping them navigate one of the most challenging times in their lives. In doing so, you'll not only make a lasting impact on the families you serve but also find satisfaction and financial success in your work. Mary's story serves as a powerful example of how a service-oriented mindset can lead to incredible growth and achievement in any sales environment.

For a fun visual on the concept of Service over Sales, visit: sellingwithsensitivity.com/bonuses

ORDER-TAKING VERSUS SELLING

In the world of sales, there is a distinct difference between order-taking and selling.

Order-taking involves passively waiting for potential clients to approach you with a clear need or request. In these cases, you simply fulfill their demand by providing the requested product or service, completing the necessary paperwork, and processing their payment. In this scenario, you haven't actively sold anything; you've merely taken an order.

As an early mentor once wisely said, "The sale doesn't begin until you hear your first 'no'." This advice has remained with me throughout my career, highlighting the importance of moving beyond mere order-taking.

In contrast, service-focused selling is a more proactive approach. It entails understanding your clients' problems and finding ways to solve them. This can be challenging, especially in deathcare, where the need is not as immediate or obvious as it is in other sectors. Unlike selling hoses, where the issue is clearcut (e.g., a leaking hose), and the need is urgent, deathcare involves "pre-need" planning, where the problem isn't felt as acutely.

To achieve success in deathcare sales, you must shift from an order-taking mindset to a service-focused selling approach. This starts with getting to know your clients and identifying their underlying concerns, even if they aren't immediately apparent. By proactively addressing these concerns and offering solutions tailored to your clients' needs, you demonstrate empathy, service, and connection.

If you're ready to leave order-taking behind and embrace service-focused selling instead, ask affirming questions as you go. A successful sale often consists of a series of affirmative responses from your client. By asking questions that elicit agreement, you can create a positive momentum in your conversation and make your clients more receptive to your proposed solutions.

This process begins with your "I help" statement, which you'll be introduced to in the next chapter. Start by getting affirmation that the problem you solve is relatable and something your prospect recognizes as an issue. For example, you might ask, "You know how planning an unexpected funeral for someone is chaotic and so much more expensive than it needs to be?" (They'll likely say "yes" and might even delve into an experience they had that relates).

By adopting a service-focused selling mentality, you can improve your effectiveness in the deathcare sales industry while also providing valuable support to your clients during a sensitive and emotional time in their lives. Remember, the sale truly begins when you hear the first "no." Your ability to address objections, offer solutions, and empathize with your clients will set you apart as a successful deathcare sales professional.

THE SALESY PARADOX

A curious aspect of our chosen career in sales is that we embrace our identity as "salespeople" yet simultaneously harbor a deep-seated fear of coming across as "salesy". I find this paradox to be both amusing and perplexing. The irony lies in the fact that, while we take pride in our profession and acknowledge the critical role we play in assisting families, we still grapple with the concern of appearing too pushy or fake.

This worry comes from the stereotype associated with sales, and the desire to prove that we are the exception to the stigma. In our line of work, we must find a balance between embracing our role as salespeople and ensuring that our approach aligns with the compassionate, empathetic nature of our industry.

Recognizing that appearing "salesy" depends entirely on *internal motivation* is key. If your main goal when meeting a family is to fatten your wallet or appease your boss by clearing out certain inventory, or if you make assumptions about their financial capabilities and change your approach as a result, your actions will likely be perceived as salesy. This sort of motivation goes against the true, service-focused nature of our work.

On the other hand, when your primary focus is on providing exceptional service by truly getting to know the family and presenting options that cater to their expressed needs and desires, there's nothing salesy about it. In fact, that's exactly what consultative selling is. This approach prioritizes the family's well-being and ensures that you are acting in *their* best interests, not your own. This aligns with the empathetic and compassionate values of the deathcare profession. By leading with service and prioritizing real connections, you can avoid the pitfalls of "salesy" and maintain the trust and respect of the families you serve.

To avoid being perceived as salesy while still effectively addressing objections and closing sales, balance sensitivity with assertiveness. Confidence and empathy go hand-in-hand when guiding families through the decision-making process.

When you sense that you're being perceived as salesy, try these exercises to recenter yourself:

1. Take a step back and a deep breath. A silent check-in with yourself is fine if you don't feel it's appropriate to physically step away.

2. Remind yourself of your true motivation—helping your client make the best decisions for their family.

3. Reaffirm your commitment to serving the family with compassion.

By recentering and maintaining your focus on the family's needs, you can feel confident that the sales methods you're using are not salesy but genuinely in service of the family.

Committing to serving families with integrity, empathy, and dedication creates a foundation for sustainable success that enriches your career, benefits you financially, and makes a meaningful difference in the lives of those you serve.

CHAPTER 6
CLIENT GENERATION

PEOPLE DON'T BUY products and services; they buy solutions. A salesperson who embraces this concept and leverages custom solutions for their clients will be much more successful than a salesperson who is pushing a product or service.

We don't have control over when we receive a call informing us that a family has lost a loved one and needs our assistance in arranging services, property, or products. Even so, it's not something we'd ever wish to manipulate, as our role is to provide compassionate support during difficult times, not to create difficult times so that we can capitalize on them. Who would want to be that guy?!

We do, however, have control over our own proactive efforts to protect families from the chaos, unexpected financial burdens, and stress that can arise during an already challenging period. By offering our expertise and guidance, we can alleviate some of the strain and ensure a smoother experience during their time of need.

As we discuss marketing, our focus will be on advanced planning sales. We'll leave the negative stigma-solidification to the competitor down the street. You know who I'm talking about – the deathcare equivalent of an ambulance-chaser.

In the world of deathcare sales, particularly when you're focused on advanced planning sales, understanding your ideal client is essential for developing a targeted marketing plan. This knowledge, combined with your personal experiences, helps you create meaningful connections with potential clients. In this chapter, we'll explore how to identify your ideal client and incorporate an impactful "I help" statement into your sales strategy.

IDENTIFYING YOUR IDEAL CLIENT

In the realm of marketing, not everyone will be the perfect fit for your products or services. Trying to cater to everyone's needs can spread your resources too thin, dilute your message, and diminish your impact. By identifying your ideal client, you can focus your efforts on those who are most likely to benefit from what you offer. This will result in more efficient and effective marketing campaigns.

Start by defining your ideal client based on who you are passionate about helping. In many cases, we tend to target a previous version of ourselves. Do you find that to be true? Use your personal experiences to understand your target audience better. For example, if you have faced the challenges of planning a funeral without prior arrangements, you may be motivated to help others avoid that stress. Your story of losing a loved one and dealing with the uncertainty of their final wishes may resonate with people in similar situations, helping you connect with them on a deeper level.

If you are specifically targeting local demographics, you may be focusing on women aged 55 and above, senior couples, grandparents, parents of high-school-aged children, or middle-aged men who have lost one or both of their parents. The possibilities are endless when it comes to narrowing down your ideal client. Personally, I have always enjoyed the process of developing my ideal client—it feels like creating a character in a novel.

Once you have identified your ideal clients, delve into their habits and preferences to determine where they spend their time and the problems they face. By positioning yourself as a helpful resource in the places they frequent, you can engage them in a familiar environment and start conversations about end-of-life planning.

For instance, if your ideal clients attend community events or visit local farmers' markets, consider setting up a booth or offering a workshop to reach them in a relaxed setting. If they primarily use one social media platform, focus your marketing efforts there.

Remember, this process is not about speaking your buying clients into existence... They already exist! This exercise is simply designed to help you target a specific client whose problem you can solve. It enables you to communicate with them in a relatable way that captures their attention, highlights the problem they have, and positions you as a potential solution.

To effectively communicate with your ideal clients, answer these key questions about them:

1. What makes them smile?

2. What makes them cry?

3. What keeps them up at night?

These insights will help you craft marketing messages that resonate with your target audience and demonstrate your genuine understanding of their needs. For instance, if your ideal clients are parents, you can emphasize the peace of mind that comes from having a well-planned end-of-life strategy in place and the importance of avoiding uncertainty for their family's future.

In the deathcare industry, advanced planning sales often require a proactive approach, as many clients may not yet have recognized the problem of planning for end-of-life events. In Western society, we tend to compartmentalize all things death into the "later" category. We don't want to think about it, much less talk about it. If we don't want to talk about it, we certainly don't want to consider spending money on it! This can be one of the most challenging aspects of deathcare sales.

When you initiate a conversation, use storytelling and persuasive skills to help them recognize the problem and guide them towards a solution. Share personal anecdotes, such as your experience of losing a loved one or your experience helping a family who has lost someone, to illustrate the importance of pre-need planning and prompt your ideal client to act.

INCORPORATING AN "I HELP" STATEMENT

As you develop your understanding of your ideal client, create an "I help" statement to concisely explain your role when someone asks. This statement not only helps you communicate effectively but also ensures more engaging and meaningful conversations.

Before you launch into your "I help" statement, you need to get validation for the problem you solve with the phrase "You know how…"

"You know how when someone dies, arranging their end-of-life services can bring out the worst in some people and even tear families apart?" By starting this way, you'll make it easy for people to recognize the value of what you offer.

Once your prospect has validated that you provide a solution to a relatable problem, it's time to let them know that you are the right person to help. Your "I help" statement should:

Specify your target audience by describing your ideal client:

- *"I help Metro Detroit seniors to have peace of mind…"*
  By clearly defining who you help, you demonstrate your focus and commitment to addressing their specific needs. Even if the person you're talking to doesn't fit into that category, they probably know someone who does!

Explain the outcome or solution your services offer.

- *"…by gently guiding them through a simple process to ensure that their loved ones won't be saddled with extra emotional or financial stressors when they pass." By emphasizing the result, you highlight the benefits of your services and showcase your value.*

Describe your process for achieving the desired result for your clients.

- *"I listen to my clients' concerns, help them explore their options, and support them as they make informed decisions about their end-of-life plans." This is your opportunity to show how you're different from someone else in the same role.*

After presenting your "I help" statement, get the focus *the heck off of* you. Ask a question that redirects the conversation back to the person with whom you're speaking. This approach helps you uncover potential problems they may have, allowing you to position yourself as a problem solver rather than a salesperson.

"Have you ever had to plan an unexpected funeral for someone?" By asking this question, you invite the person to share their experiences, and you open a conversation about their family's needs.

In addition to your "I help" statement, consider sharing relatable examples or stories that illustrate the various segments of your statement. This will make your message even more engaging and help potential clients better understand the value of your services.

For example, when explaining the outcome or solution your services offer, you might share a story about a client who went through the pre-need planning process and experienced peace of mind knowing their family wouldn't have to face additional stress during a difficult time. Or, when describing your process, you could give an example of a time you helped a client explore various options for their end-of-life plan, such as selecting green burial options or deciding on mausoleum entombment.

By identifying your ideal client, understanding their needs, and incorporating an "I help" statement with illustrative examples, you can develop targeted marketing strategies that connect with them on a deeper level.

Visit sellingwithsensitivity.com/bonuses for resources on developing both your ideal client and your "I help" statement.

SENSITIVE MARKETING

The key to effective, sensitive marketing lies in adding value - and doing so at no cost to your potential client. You are in a unique position to offer knowledge, guidance, and resources that can make a world of difference to someone navigating the complexities of end-of-life planning. Offer something of value as a gentle hook that softens your ideal client to you, opening the door to deeper conversations and stronger connections.

Take a moment to brainstorm. What resources do you have at your fingertips that you could share? Even if the resources you'd like to offer don't exist yet, with a little research and creativity, you can create your own! Here are some ideas to spark your thinking:

1. Share information about what happens - and the costs associated - when someone dies without a will in your state. Providing this vital information can help families better understand the importance of advanced planning.

2. Provide your potential clients with information about what probate is and suggestions on how to keep their estate out of probate.

3. Offering a free checklist or guide to help clients navigate their first end-of-life discussions with their families can be an invaluable resource, and it helps families to avoid emotional arguments over details during an already-difficult time.

4. Compile a list of local grief resources - support groups, therapists, memorial services - and make it available to your clients. This simple gesture shows your commitment to supporting them beyond the point of sale.

As you delve into the following sections on Dusty Files and Informational Sessions, keep the concept of offering value at the forefront of your mind. The more you can assist, inform, and support potential clients, the more they will come to see you as their trusted advisor.

DUSTY FILE DIVING

Every sales role is a link in a chain, a continuation of a story written by those who have filled the role before you. You've not only inherited a position but also a collection of relationships, a history of interactions, and a legacy of sorts. These family files, records, or "dusty leads," so to speak, can seem initially overwhelming. But with the right perspective and approach, they can become a gold mine of client generation opportunities. Let's explore how you can dive into these files to reconnect, add value, and serve these inherited contacts effectively.

Think of these family files as treasure chests filled with relationships that may have been forgotten or neglected. These files can offer you a starting point, a way to reconnect with past clients and see if they or their extended family might benefit from your services. This is a way to reaffirm relationships and remind families you're there to serve them, even if some time has passed since their last contact. Service, trust, and longevity are key in deathcare sales. These aren't one-off customers; these are relationships built over time and across generations.

Use the three-step system below to turn your dusty leads into a pipeline of warm connections and a reservoir of potential referrals.

Organize. Begin by structuring your inherited family files or archives systematically. This organization could be based on date, client's last name, or service type. The goal is to simplify your search process and increase your efficiency.

Analyze. Once your files are organized, devote a part of your day to reviewing them. Search for unfulfilled needs and opportunities for follow-up. If a preplanned client's spouse isn't part of the package, that's an opportunity. If a preplanned client has living parents but they haven't preplanned yet, that's an opportunity. If they've preplanned part of their services but not all, that's an opportunity. If a family seemingly has everything already planned in advance, reach out anyway. Clients who believe in the power of advanced planning are a great resource for referrals. Every file is a treasure chest of information waiting to be unlocked.

Reconnect. Crafting a sensitive and thoughtful outreach strategy is critical. When reconnecting with "dusty" leads, remember the purpose of your call isn't to sell but to provide value, build a relationship, and understand their needs better. Here are a few reasons to make that call:

1. Anniversary of a death or special day: A thoughtful message on the anniversary of a loved one's death, birthday, or special day can show your potential client that you care and that they're not alone in remembering.

––––––

Every year, the rhythm of my Facebook memories is broken by a poignant post I made a week after Dad died. It reads, "Life goes on, even when it doesn't feel like it should." As I reflect on that message year after year, I'm transported back to that period of profound lone-liness, to the sensation of my world standing still while everyone else's seemingly spun forward into normalcy. How was it that life could move on so easily?

In the aftermath of losing Dad, it was unsettling how that shift to normalcy came so easily to the people around me. As the world around me started to regain its regular rhythm, I found myself drifting, wondering if I was the only one who remembered, the only one still feeling the sting of Dad's absence.

But then something happened on the day before my first Father's Day without Dad. In the midst of what was a pretty tough weekend, I received a card in the mail. Not just any card, but a heartfelt note from a friend. It was a simple thing, but it meant so much. She'd taken the time to let me know she was thinking about me on my first Father's Day without my father.

More than that, it was a reminder that Dad's memory was alive in others, and not just in me. Her kindness reminded me that even though my world had shifted, there were still people out there who remembered Dad, and who cared. It's those little moments, those seemingly small acts, that can really make a difference when someone is trying to navigate the tidal wave of grief.

———

2. Invitation to an Event: If you're hosting a community event, seminar, or special service, extend an invitation to your potential client. This lets them know that you consider them to be a part of your community.

3. File Review: Let your potential client know that you're updating your records and want to confirm that their information is still current. This is an excellent opportunity to re-establish communication and ensure that the family is aware of your most up-to-date offerings that may not have been available when they last spoke with your organization.

There's a sneaky little trap that tends to catch those new to dusty file diving, and it's all about balance. It's way too easy to get lost in the first two-thirds of this three-step system, devoting all your energy to organizing and analyzing. But that's not where the magic happens! The real business-building happens during outreach when you're building those connections.

So, here's the trick: Do your homework, but don't let it take over. Gather enough gems from your research to make your outreach meaningful, but don't let the pre-call preparation hold you hostage. It's time to act! Pick up the phone and make the call. It's all about breathing new life into those dormant leads, turning them into vibrant connections and a fruitful network of potential referrals. Ready, set, dial!

INFORMATIONAL SESSIONS

While dusty file diving allows us to reconnect with people who already have a vested interest in what we do, thanks to previous relationships with us or our predecessors, information sessions open an entirely new chapter. Here, we seek to ignite the spark of interest among individuals and families we've never had the privilege to serve before. It's about extending our reach, building new bridges, and introducing our invaluable services to a fresh audience. These gatherings are a prime opportunity to let our community know who we are, what we do, and how we can help them when they need it most. So, let's roll up our sleeves and prepare to engage our community in a whole new way.

1. **Identify your audience**. Consider which local businesses, organizations, and professionals could derive benefit from an informational session. Potential fields include elder law,

estate planning, retirement communities, churches, and finan-cial advisors.

2. Prepare engaging content. Develop a presentation that provides real value and demonstrates your experience. Ensure your material is both informative and engaging, emphasizing the importance of end-of-life advanced planning.

3. Promote and execute. Strategically market your information sessions to your identified audience and execute them effectively. By providing knowledge and a safe space for questions, you position yourself as a trusted resource in your field.

In addition, utilize consistent, inexpensive, personal options like spending an hour each week at a local restaurant for a cup of coffee. Share this casual event on social media, speaking directly to your ideal client base. Even if you spend many of these hours alone, you're showing your potential clients that you're consistently available to offer valuable information over a casual cup of coffee when they're ready. This is a great way to incorporate social media marketing into your business.

Every interaction is a step toward building trust and credibility. Keep the focus on adding value, and you'll find yourself becoming the go-to person in your community.

CHAPTER 7
UNDERSTANDING GRIEF

THE STAGES OF GRIEF

WHILE GRIEF IS A HIGHLY individualized process, many people go through a series of emotions as they cope with their loss. The well-known Kübler-Ross model, also known as the five stages of grief, includes denial, anger, bargaining, depression, and acceptance.

Denial: In the initial stage of grief, a bereaved person—much like I was when my dad died—may have difficulty accepting the reality of their loved one's death. They might think there's been a mistake, that their loved one is still alive, or that they'll wake up to find it was all a bad dream. During this stage, you should be patient and allow the individual time to process the news and gradually come to terms with the reality of the situation, just as I had to when I found Dad.

Anger: As the reality of the loss sets in, a grieving person may experience feelings of anger and resentment. They may direct their anger towards themselves, others or even the deceased loved one for leaving them behind. In my case, I grappled with anger towards the situation and the overwhelming responsibilities that followed. I also found myself angry at my dad for not making an effort ahead of time to lessen my responsibility load once he died. In this stage, you, as a death-care professional, must provide a safe space for the bereaved to express their emotions without judgment.

Bargaining: In the bargaining stage, the grieving person might try to make deals with a higher power to reverse the loss or lessen the pain. They may have thoughts like, "If only I had done this differently, maybe my loved one would still be here." You can help by acknowledging the person's feelings and gently guiding them towards more constructive coping mechanisms.

Depression: As the full impact of the loss becomes clearer, the grieving individual may feel intense sadness and hopelessness. I recall the difficulties I faced as the only child and decision-maker, burdened with both financial and emotional responsibilities. It is crucial during this stage to be sensitive to their emotional state and provide resources for support, such as grief counseling or support groups. Additionally, offer a compassionate and attentive ear, allowing them to express their feelings and thoughts.

Acceptance: In the final stage of grief, the bereaved begins to accept the reality of their loved one's death and starts to look for a path forward. They may start making plans and finding new ways to honor their loved one's memory. At this stage, you can help by offering options and guidance for memorialization and services that reflect the individual's wishes and the family's needs.

It's important to note that healing is not linear. Those grappling with grief may move between different stages without a specific order, and sometimes even experience multiple stages within a short span of time, sometimes in just a matter of seconds. By recognizing these stages and the accompanying emotions, you can customize your approach to better address the needs of grieving clients. This will allow you to provide support in a sensitive and empathetic manner, understanding the complexities of their journey.

In my years of working with grieving individuals and families, I've witnessed the intricate dance of emotions that accompanies the grieving process. As I often remind my team, "Grief plays dress-up, and its favorite costume is anger." This poignant reminder captures the essence of how grief manifests itself, camouflaging its true nature and making it challenging to navigate.

———

I'll never forget the first person who brought me to tears in the deathcare industry. His name was Oliver. He and his wife, May, had been middle-school sweethearts and married right after high school. Sixty-two years, three children, and several grandchildren later, May was losing her battle with cancer. Oliver visited the cemetery to make arrangements for both of them, hoping those arrangements wouldn't be needed for many years to come. During our time together, I discovered that Oliver had been good friends with my grandfather. He shared stories of their youthful antics, which I loved. Oliver arranged final resting places inside a mausoleum for himself and May. Sadly, less than a month later, May passed away and was laid to rest.

Oliver visited daily. One afternoon, while I was assisting a family at a satellite office, Oliver stopped by the main office with a question for me. He was furious that I wasn't available to speak with him at that moment. His grief quickly morphed into anger, and during his visit, he had an outburst, which involved shoving one of my male coworkers and challenging him to "take it outside like men."

By the time I could call to speak with him, a couple of hours had passed. Those fifteen minutes felt like an eternity as I endured a barrage of berating and insulting comments. To make matters worse, since he knew my grandfather, he added more biting remarks about how I had brought shame to my grandfather's name and how disappointed Grandpa would be if he could see me now. I silently cried as I listened, partly because his words were hurtful but mostly because I could feel the immense pain he was experiencing after losing the love of his life.

––––––

Grief can present itself in numerous forms, often masquerading as different emotions. Among many grieving individuals, anger becomes a prevalent emotion when dealing with deathcare facilities and professionals. This is because anger can give them a sense of productivity, making them feel like they are actively fighting for their loved ones, even when their true emotions are rooted in sadness and loss.

When confronted with grief masked as anger, it is important to practice *responsive* rather than *reactive* behavior. Our initial instinct might be to become defensive, but we must recognize the underlying emotions and respond with empathy and understanding. By taking a moment to pause and consider the perspective of the bereaved person, we can better tailor our response to their specific needs and offer the support and resources they require. This approach fosters a compassionate environment where families feel heard and cared for, ultimately contributing to a more positive experience during this immensely challenging time.

CULTURAL AND PERSONAL FACTORS IN GRIEVING

Cultural Practices: Every culture has its unique customs and practices related to death and mourning. For example, some cultures may have specific rituals surrounding the preparation of the deceased's body, while others may have particular ceremonies to honor the deceased. In certain traditions, the mourning period may last for a set number of days, and specific rituals or prayers may be performed at designated times. Understanding these cultural practices is vital for deathcare sales professionals to provide appropriate support and services tailored to the needs and expectations of each family.

Religious Beliefs: Religion often plays a significant role in how individuals and families process grief and navigate the deathcare process. Different religious traditions may have unique beliefs about the afterlife, funeral rites, and mourning practices. Deathcare sales professionals should familiarize themselves with various religious customs and be prepared to accommodate the needs and requests of families from diverse religious backgrounds.

Personal Beliefs and Preferences: Beyond cultural and religious practices, individuals may have their own personal beliefs and preferences when it comes to death and mourning. These beliefs may be shaped by factors such as personal experiences with loss, family traditions, or individual values. Some people may prefer a more private and intimate mourning process, while others may find comfort in more elaborate and public rituals. Deathcare sales professionals should be sensitive to these personal preferences and be prepared to adapt their approach accordingly.

Grieving Styles: Grieving styles can vary greatly among individuals. Some people may express their grief openly, sharing their emotions and seeking support from others, while others may adopt a more reserved approach, processing their feelings internally. It is important to be sensitive to these different grieving styles and adapt your communication methods accordingly to provide the best support for each family member's needs.

The Importance of Cultural Competency: To better serve grieving families, strive to develop cultural competency, which refers to the ability to understand, communicate with, and effectively interact with people across cultures. This involves being aware of one's own cultural biases and assumptions, seeking knowledge about different cultural practices and beliefs, and developing the skills to communicate respectfully and effectively across cultural differences. By fostering cultural competency, deathcare sales professionals can create a more inclusive and supportive environment for families coping with loss.

By familiarizing yourself with the stages of grief, recognizing the emotions that accompany them, and being sensitive to cultural, religious, and personal factors, you can better serve grieving families and provide the support they need during difficult times.

CHAPTER 8
CRAFTING A COMPELLING SALES PITCH

EMOTION FIRST, THEN LOGIC

IN ADVANCED END-OF-LIFE SALES, you must consider the perspective through your client's eyes. Death-care purchases are primarily driven by emotions before logic comes into play.

Emotion-First Chain of Thought: *I love this Taj Mahal-esque private mausoleum option, and I can see generations of my family coming to visit. I love that I can keep my family together and maybe even bring my deceased grandparents over from another cemetery to include them in the family estate. This location feels peaceful, and I particularly love the way the sun shines through those tree branches to provide a little shade to whoever is visiting. Oh, also, I can memorialize with a favorite bible verse and custom emblem for every family member to make sure their memorials all really envelop who they were.*

Then Logic: *How can I make this work financially?*

Your role is to help clients explore different financial options to make their preferred choice work for them. Leading with emotion rather than logic will create a different client experience.

Logic First: *I've seen the least expensive options, and they're fine. I don't really need anything nicer than that.*

Emotion-Second Chain of Thought: *As much as I hate the idea of being in the ground - because of bugs and water - it's less expensive than the mausoleum option. I just won't think about the ick factor of being in the ground. That mausoleum was beautiful, but I'm sure it's just for rich people, not people like me. I wonder what life would have been like if I'd _____ instead of taking the career path I did. I bet I'd have been able to give my family better in life and in death. I bet I'd be able to be in the mausoleum. I feel like a failure.*

The emotion-then-logic aspect should be considered when presenting different options and guiding clients through the decision-making process. Here are some strategies to help you effectively engage with clients on an emotional level:

1. Ask about feelings, not just thoughts: Encourage clients to share their feelings rather than merely analyze the details. Instead of asking, "What do you think about this plan?" ask, "How does this plan feel to you?" This approach keeps clients in an emotional frame of mind, allowing them to connect more deeply with their choices.

2. Use personal examples and stories: To highlight the impact of pre-need planning on families, consider sharing anecdotes, personal experiences, or client stories. These narratives can evoke powerful emotions and enable clients to visualize the benefits of your offerings for their loved ones. Sharing your own journey, such as the experience of losing a loved one unexpectedly without any prior arrangements, can resonate deeply with many families. It can help them understand the importance of proactive end-of-life planning and motivate them to act for the well-being of their own families.

3. Make it personal: When discussing plans, use the names of the people who will be affected by the client's decisions. For example, say, "Can you see why it will be beneficial for your daughter Suzie to have this booklet full of your wishes?" or "Can you imagine Suzie standing here by the pond with her kids when they visit?" Personalizing the conversation in this way helps clients visualize the emotional benefits of their choices.

4. Present top-down, not bottom-up: When presenting options to families, show the nicest options first. Presenting bottom-up may cause families to justify the less expensive options right away, making them feel like you're trying to upsell them into nicer options as you continue. When you work top-down, you're allowing their emotion to lead the way. Your goal is to find the family's true desire for their end-of-life plan and then see if you can make the financial piece doable for them.

5. *Make* **it work financially:** If a family has developed a strong attachment to a plan that exceeds their comfortable price range, it is important to think creatively about how you can assist them. One option is to explore the possibility of extending financing for an additional year or two, which would help keep the monthly payments at a more affordable level. If you are already utilizing the most generous financing options available, consider breaking down the purchase into smaller components. Identify the most essential element that the family needs to secure now to ensure their vision can be realized. If the monthly payment for that component is manageable, they can gradually add any additional elements in the future once the initial payment has been completed. This approach allows the family to work towards their vision in a way that aligns with their financial capabilities.

6. Validate emotions: Acknowledge and validate the emotions your clients express during the decision-making process. End-of-life planning can be an emotional experience for many, and showing empathy and understanding will help build trust and rapport.

7. Take your time: Allow clients to process their emotions and make decisions at their own pace. Rushing them through the process may cause them to feel overwhelmed or pressured, which can hinder their ability to make emotionally informed choices.

8. Offer support: Be a source of support and guidance for clients as they navigate the emotional journey of end-of-life planning. Offer resources, such as counseling or support groups, that can help them cope with their feelings and make more informed decisions.

To effectively guide clients through the emotionally charged decision-making process of end-of-life planning, it is important to prioritize emotions before addressing logic. By connecting with clients on an emotional level and providing personalized support, you can help them make choices that truly resonate with them. This approach acknowledges the deep emotional impact of end-of-life decisions and allows you to offer guidance and assistance that is sensitive to their individual needs and desires. By focusing on emotions first and then integrating logical considerations, you will be better equipped to support clients in making decisions that align with their values and bring them a sense of peace and fulfillment.

FEATURES AND BENEFITS

When developing a compelling sales pitch, it's essential to understand the difference between features and benefits. While features describe the product or service's characteristics, benefits focus on the value these characteristics bring to the customer. To truly engage with your clients and create a persuasive sales pitch, you must emphasize the benefits of your offerings rather than merely listing features.

Features are the facts about your product or service: its size, color, materials, functions, and so on. While these details are important, they don't necessarily resonate with your clients on an emotional level. Benefits, on the other hand, are the positive outcomes your clients will experience as a result of using your product or service. They demonstrate how your offerings will improve their lives, fulfill their needs, and solve their problems.

For example, in the deathcare industry, a feature of a pre-need plan might be "flexible payment options." The corresponding benefit would be "peace of mind knowing your family won't be burdened with unexpected funeral costs." By focusing on the benefit, you tap into your clients' emotions and help them envision the value your product or service will bring to their lives.

To create a compelling sales pitch, follow these steps:

1. Identify the key features of your product or service.

2. For each feature, determine the corresponding benefit.

3. Craft your pitch to emphasize these benefits, using emotional language and storytelling to create a connection with your clients.

Remember, your clients are likely to be more interested in what your product or service can do for them than in the product or service itself. By focusing on benefits rather than features, you demonstrate that you understand their needs and desires and position your offerings as the solution to their problems. This approach will make your sales pitch more persuasive and also help you build trust and rapport with your clients, ultimately fostering long-lasting relationships.

STORYTELLING

One of the most powerful tools you can use in your sales pitch is storytelling. Humans are innately drawn to stories, as they evoke emotions, create connections, and make complex ideas easier to understand. By incorporating storytelling into your sales pitch, you can engage your clients on a deeper level, capture their attention, and make your message more memorable.

To create a compelling story, you need to include three key elements:

1. A relatable character. Your story should feature a character that your audience can relate to and see themselves in. This could be a client, a family member, or even yourself. By creating a connection between your audience and the character, you can draw them into the story and make them more emotionally invested in the outcome.

2. Conflict or challenge. Introduce a problem or challenge that the character must overcome. This conflict should be relevant to your product or service, illustrating the need for your offering or the benefits it can provide. By presenting a challenge, you can create tension and intrigue that will keep your audience engaged.

3. Resolution. Wrap up your story by showing how the character resolves the conflict or overcomes the challenge. This is your opportunity to demonstrate the value of your product or service and leave a lasting impression on your audience. Be sure to emphasize the emotional impact of the resolution, as this will help your audience connect with your message on a personal level.

In the deathcare industry, storytelling can be particularly impactful, as it allows you to address sensitive topics and demonstrate the real-life benefits of your offerings. By sharing stories of families who have experienced the peace of mind that comes from pre-planning, for example, you can help your clients envision the positive impact your services could have on their own lives.

Remember, stories have the power to create connections, evoke emotions, and inspire action. By incorporating story-telling into your sales pitch, you can make your message more compelling and memorable, ultimately leading to greater success in your sales efforts.

By prioritizing emotion and then incorporating logic, emphasizing the benefits rather than just the features, and utilizing powerful storytelling, you can create a pitch that deeply resonates with clients and effectively showcases the value of your services. Implementing these strategies will not only enhance your sales success but also establish enduring relationships and provide genuine support for families as they navigate the complex and emotional realm of end-of-life planning.

CHAPTER 9
OVERCOMING OBJECTIONS AND CLOSING THE SALE

SALES QUIZ...

Q: When is the best time to overcome an objection?

A: Before it comes!

Addressing potential objections before they even arise can help to eliminate concerns and establish trust with your clients.

Anticipating and addressing common objections is a key component of successful sales interactions. By proactively addressing potential concerns, you can create an environment of understanding and trust, making it easier for clients to make decisions.

Addressing Anticipated Objections When Setting Appointments

When trying to set appointments, be prepared to overcome anticipated objections by knowing that among the most common objections are feeling obligated or pressured to purchase something and worrying about the time commitment involved in attending the appointment. To overcome these objections, consider the following strategies:

1. Reassure them of your intentions: Assure families that your primary goal is to provide information and support without any pressure or obligation. Emphasize your role as a resource and a compassionate guide rather than a salesperson.

2. Offer a no-pressure approach: Make it clear that you understand their concerns and that you will not push them into making any decisions during the appointment. Instead, focus on providing them with valuable information and resources that will help them make informed decisions on their own terms.

3. Be transparent about time commitment: Be upfront about the expected duration of the appointment. Inform them that you will be respectful of their time and will work efficiently to cover the necessary topics while also leaving room for their questions and concerns.

4. Highlight the benefits of the appointment: Explain the advantages of attending the appointment, such as gaining a better understanding of their options, receiving personalized recommendations, and having the opportunity to ask questions in a comfortable, one-on-one setting.

5. Offer flexibility: Provide families with several options for scheduling an appointment, including different dates, times, and locations. Standard location options include your office or their home but get creative! If they're comfortable at the local library or coffee shop, offer to meet them there instead! This flexibility demonstrates your willingness to accommodate their needs and comfort and helps to alleviate concerns about time commitment.

6. Reinforce your empathy: Remind them that you understand the challenges they are currently facing and that your priority is to support them during this difficult time. Reiterate that you are there to help and provide guidance, not to pressure them into making decisions with which they are uncomfortable.

As you engage with more potential clients to discuss their end-of-life arrangements, it is possible that you will encounter additional common objections that arise as significant concerns. To effectively address these anticipated objections, it is important to be proactive and adapt your appointment-setting conversations accordingly. Regularly review and refine your approach to ensure that you are effectively meeting the needs and addressing the concerns of the families you serve. By doing so, you can enhance your ability to address objections, establish trust, and provide the necessary support for individuals and families during the end-of-life planning process.

ADDRESSING ANTICIPATED OBJECTIONS IN YOUR PRESENTATION AND INTERACTION

To effectively overcome objections before they arise, incorporate responses to these concerns into your presentation and interactions with clients. You can do this in a few ways:

1. **Clarity:** Be clear and concise in your presentation, addressing the most common objections in a way that is informative and easy to understand. Provide relevant examples and stories that illustrate how your product or service has helped others in similar situations.

2. **Value:** Highlight the value of your offering and emphasize the benefits it can bring to the client. This can help to alleviate concerns about cost and show that your product or service is worth the investment.

3. **Flexibility:** Offer options and alternatives to cater to different budgets and individual needs. By presenting a range of possibilities, you can show clients that you understand their concerns and are willing to work with them to find the best solution.

4. **Trust:** Build trust by being genuine, transparent, and professional in all your interactions. Show clients that you are

dedicated to their well-being and are committed to providing the support they need.

By addressing objections proactively, you can create an environment of understanding and trust, making it easier for clients to move forward in their decision-making process.

ADDRESSING OBJECTIONS AS THEY ARISE

Despite your best efforts to address anticipated objections proactively, clients will likely still voice concerns during your interactions. In these situations, you must (a) approach their objections with respect, understanding, and patience, and (b) have the courage to *not* simply back out of the conversation. Let's look at three of the most common objections and how to effectively overcome them:

"We have to talk to our kids before we make a decision to move forward."

First, acknowledge their concern. Express understanding and emphasize the importance of involving the family in the decision-making process.

Next, offer a different perspective. Remind them that throughout their lives, they have made countless decisions for their children's well-being without seeking their permission, such as going to work every day, cooking dinner each night, or choosing birthday and holiday gifts. Frame the end-of-life planning as the final act of parenting, a gift that they can give to their children to alleviate the burden of making these arrangements in the future. This perspective highlights the selflessness and love behind their decision.

Then, let them know that discussing their plans with their children can prevent potential misunderstandings and conflicts in the future and that you wholeheartedly encourage it. However, prepare them for the possibility that their children may not want to engage in the conversation. Explain that this reluctance is not because advance planning is a bad idea but because it forces individuals to confront uncomfortable thoughts and emotions. By acknowledging this, you can help them understand the challenges that may arise in discussing their plans and still emphasize the importance of open communication.

Ensure that throughout, you're using their children's names to create a more personal and emotionally resonant connection. This approach helps to emphasize the "emotion first, then logical" nature of end-of-life advanced planning and demonstrates that you understand their motivations and priorities.

By adjusting your response to emphasize the emotional connection and positioning advanced end-of-life planning as a final act of love, you can effectively address the concerns of potential clients. Highlight the significance of planning ahead to care for their loved ones and ensure their wishes are respected. By framing the conversation in this manner, you can guide them towards a confident decision-making process, emphasizing the importance of taking proactive steps to provide peace of mind for both them and their families.

"It's too expensive."

As with any objection, begin by empathizing with their concern. Acknowledge that financial concerns are valid and that investing in end-of-life planning can be a significant expense.

Then, keep emotion at the forefront. Rather than offering discounts or trying to make the numbers fit, maintain the focus on the emotional aspects of end-of-life planning. Assuming you have built rapport with the family, learned about their loved ones, and understand who they wish to protect, you can use the "too expensive" objection to emphasize the importance of taking care of it in advance, so their kids won't be saddled with the expenses on a day that will already prove to be possibly the most challenging of their lives.

Present a comparison of the costs of planning now versus waiting 10, 20, or 30 years or not planning at all, which would leave their children with the financial obligation upon their deaths.

Discuss various financing and payment plans available for pre-planning their end-of-life arrangements. This can help make the costs more manageable and accessible while still addressing their financial concerns.

By staying confident in the value of what you are offering and focusing on emotion and the long-term benefits of end-of-life planning, you can effectively address the "It's too expensive" objection while maintaining a strong connection with your clients and guiding them towards a decision that best suits their financial situation and preferences.

"I have life insurance that will pay for everything."

First, validate the value of life insurance and offer kudos to your family on having arranged for the insurance to protect their family. Recognize the importance of life insurance in providing financial security for their loved ones.

Next, clarify the purpose of life insurance. Explain that life insurance is typically meant to replace the lost income and cover living expenses for the beneficiaries rather than specifically covering end-of-life expenses. For example, consider the lost income that occurs upon death. A $100,000 life insurance policy will cover 2 years of a $50,000 annual salary that is lost with a loved one's passing. If end-of-life arrangements are taken out of that policy, that's even less time that those left behind will have the financial support that they need to continue to cover daily expenses.

Finally, it is important to explain that advanced planning is designed to complement their life insurance policy, ensuring that their end-of-life expenses are covered without burdening their family financially. Waiting until the time of need can result in significantly higher costs, often more than double the original price. This can place a greater strain on the life insurance payout, leaving fewer funds available to manage the family's ongoing living expenses. By emphasizing the potential financial consequences of postponing planning, you can help clients understand the importance of taking action sooner rather than later to protect their loved ones' financial well-being.

Addressing objections as they arise is a crucial aspect of deathcare sales. By maintaining a strong emotional connection, empathizing with your clients, and confidently presenting the long-term benefits of end-of-life planning, you can effectively navigate these challenging conversations.

Remember to validate their concerns, offer alternative perspectives, and focus on the importance of empathy, service, and connection throughout the entire process. By doing so, you will not only help your clients make informed decisions but also strengthen your relationship with them, ultimately leading to more successful outcomes in your deathcare sales endeavors.

CREATING A SENSE OF URGENCY

Balance the need for compassionate support with the necessity of making timely decisions. Creating a sense of urgency can help families move forward in the decision-making process without feeling overwhelmed or pressured. Here are some strategies for fostering a sense of urgency while maintaining a sensitive approach:

Communicate Deadlines: Clearly communicate any deadlines or time constraints associated with the decision-making process, such as submission deadlines for insurance claims, scheduling constraints for funeral services, or required timelines for estate planning. Providing this information helps families understand the importance of making timely decisions without feeling unduly pressured.

Highlight Time-Sensitive Opportunities: If time-sensitive options or benefits are available, such as limited-time discounts, special promotions, or priority access to services, highlight these opportunities to encourage families to act promptly. Ensure that you present these options in a tactful and respectful manner without making families feel pressured or rushed.

Offer Support and Guidance: Offer your assistance and expertise throughout the decision-making process, providing support and guidance as needed. By being available to answer questions, address concerns, and provide recommendations, you can help families navigate the process more efficiently and make well-informed decisions in a timely manner.

Emphasize the Benefits of Timely Action: Discuss the benefits of making prompt decisions, such as reducing stress, ensuring access to preferred services or products, and allowing more time for grieving and healing or for living stress-free. Focusing on the positive outcomes associated with timely action can encourage families to move forward in the decision-making process.

Share Personal Stories or Testimonials: Share personal stories or testimonials from other families who have benefited from acting promptly in similar situations. This can provide motivation and encouragement for families to make timely decisions while also demonstrating your understanding of their unique challenges and concerns.

———

One of the most impactful stories I share when addressing objections highlights the serious consequences of inaction. Early in my career in the deathcare industry, I encountered Allison, an eighty-something retired teacher.

One Saturday morning, Allison visited the cemetery office and introduced herself, asking about an available gravesite next to her dear friend, Richelle, who had already been laid to rest. They had been friends since kindergarten, and Allison was pleased to learn that the adjacent space was available. She knew she didn't want to be cremated and confirmed that the spot was suitable for a casket burial. Allison's husband had passed away when she was in her twenties and was buried out of state. She wished to be interred next to Richelle, who had supported her for decades after she lost her husband, and so her local children and future generations could visit. However, Allison hesitated to make advance arrangements, insisting that her six-figure life insurance policy would suffice and that her children knew what to do.

Allison often dropped by to chat during her visits to Richelle's grave. I grew fond of her company and looked forward to our conversations. Each time, she would inquire if the space beside Richelle was still available but never took the necessary steps to reserve it for herself. "I have a six-figure life insurance policy, and my kids know what to do," she would repeat before leaving with a smile and a wave.

Eventually, her visits ceased.

Concerned, I called Allison's home after a few weeks, only to learn from her daughter that she had recently passed away. I expressed my deepest condolences and made sure to let her daughter know that the gravesite next to Richelle was still available, offering my assistance to honor Allison's wishes.

To my dismay, her daughter replied, "Oh, we've already had her cremated and sent to Rhode Island to be scattered." My heart broke for Allison — this was not what she wanted at all.

This poignant story serves as a powerful tool to overcome objections, as it highlights the potential consequences of not addressing end-of-life arrangements in advance. It demonstrates the importance of clear communication, planning, and taking action to ensure one's final wishes are honored. While a "happily ever after" story may be comforting, the emotional impact of Allison's story offers a compelling reminder of the urgency and significance of making end-of-life decisions.

. . .

This real-life example serves to motivate individuals to face their objections head-on, prioritize their wishes, and take the necessary steps to secure the outcome they desire.

———

By anticipating and addressing objections during appointments and presentations, empathizing with clients' concerns, navigating price objections, and creating a sense of urgency, you can effectively address potential roadblocks and help clients make informed decisions.

Remember, your goal is to build trust, provide valuable information, and tailor your approach to each client's unique needs and circumstances. By mastering these techniques, you will close more sales and build lasting relationships with families, making a meaningful difference in their lives.

CHAPTER 10
FOSTERING LONG-TERM RELATIONSHIPS

TURNING COMPLAINTS INTO SALES OPPORTUNITIES

OPPORTUNITIES FOR GROWTH and connection can be found in unexpected places. While complaints may initially appear to be the antithesis of sales opportunities, they possess the potential to become powerful catalysts for building lasting relationships that generate many sales prospects. By embracing complaints as opportunities for growth and actively working to address them, you can resolve specific issues and leave even the angriest of clients grateful for your service and lay the foundation for long-term client satisfaction and loyalty.

––––––

One Saturday at the cemetery office, Carol came in seeking information about a decoration rule. Before I could address her question, she began expressing her frustration and disappointment with a recent change in the decoration policy.

Her obscenity-filled rant was palpable. I could see the grief driving her emotions as she mentioned that her husband, George, had passed away 14 weeks prior.

I listened patiently and answered her concerns calmly. I apologized for her frustration, empathized with her, and made sure she had the most up-to-date decoration policy. I took her email address so that she'd be among the first to receive any notifications of changes in the future.

During our conversation, I invited her to attend an upcoming event offered by the cemetery for the recently bereaved. In her heightened emotional state, she angrily declined the invitation.

As she prepared to leave, I asked if it would be okay to give her a hug. Tearfully, she nodded, and we embraced. She sobbed into my shoulder, allowing her emotions to flow freely.

After Carol left, I couldn't shake the feeling of her profound pain. I decided to put together a small care package for her, including a Christmas ornament featuring a poem about missing a loved one during the holidays, and a few other thoughtful items.

I wrote a heartfelt card, explaining how she had touched my heart and that I was thinking of her. I delivered the gift bag to her front porch that evening on my way home from work.

The following morning, I found a voicemail from Carol at work. She thanked me for my kindness and shared a story about how George had given her a custom Christmas ornament every year since they'd started dating more than thirty years earlier.

She had been dreading the upcoming holiday season without him but felt that the ornament I gave her was a message from him, letting her know that she would be all right.

To my surprise, she chose to attend the cemetery event I had invited her to, and she continued to participate in following events month after month. Carol has not only become a consistent source of business referrals for the cemetery, but she has also transformed into an invaluable support for others grieving the loss of their spouses.

As of this book's publication, Carol consistently offers comfort to fellow widows and widowers at cemetery events, embracing them warmly as they weep on her shoulder.

———

Remember the concept that *grief plays dress-up and its favorite costume is anger* from Chapter 7 when dealing with complaints. When a family encounters an unexpected situation, such as a policy change or a crooked tree near their loved one's grave, it can immediately trigger grief, no matter how long it's been since their loved one died.

In such moments, anger can become the most accessible outlet for their grief, as it is often easier to express and manage than the raw emotions associated with loss.

In these situations, it is crucial for you to *respond* rather than *react* to the anger. Reacting may escalate the situation and damage the relationship, whereas responding with empathy and understanding can help defuse the situation and reaffirm your commitment to supporting the family.

Keep the "grief plays dress-up" concept in mind and follow these three steps to better navigate emotionally charged situations:

1. Apologize: When a client brings up an issue or concern, the first step is to apologize sincerely, regardless of whether you believe the complaint is valid. This shows the client that you value their feelings and are willing to listen to their concerns. Apologizing can sometimes be difficult for deathcare professionals, especially when we feel as if the anger is being targeted directly at us. Be sure to understand that, although you may not personally be to blame, you are apologizing on behalf of your organization and what they're experiencing is unpleasant.

2. Empathize: Remember, the love that your client has for their loved one hasn't faded, no matter how long they've been gone. That crooked tree they're complaining about is hanging over the 9' x 3' space that is all they have left of the person they love more than anything in the world. So, while a "crooked tree" complaint may seem superfluous to you, put yourself in the client's shoes and try to understand their perspective. Empathizing with their situation demonstrates that you genuinely care about their feelings and are committed to addressing their concerns.

3. Take Action: After expressing apologies and empathy towards the client, reassure them that you will take action to address their concerns. Taking action does not necessarily mean immediately solving their problem, but rather it entails steps such as gathering more information, discussing the issue with colleagues, or conducting further investigation. The key is to communicate your intentions clearly and ensure that you follow through on your promises. Specify a day and time when they can expect to hear back from you, and make sure to follow up even if you don't have an immediate answer or solution. If this is the case, inform them that you are actively working on it and provide another specific day and time when they can anticipate a call from you. This demonstrates your integrity and builds trust with the family, showing them that you are dedicated to resolving their concerns.

By following these three steps, you can turn complaints and inquiries into opportunities to build rapport with your clients. This approach allows you to address their concerns in a compassionate and sensitive manner, ultimately fostering a strong, long-term relationship.

For an additional resource on this three-step process to handling complaints, visit sellingwithsensitivity.com/ bonuses

FOLLOWING UP

Following up with clients is an essential part of fostering long-term relationships in the deathcare industry. Consistent communication and engagement show that you genuinely care about the well-being of the families you serve, even after services have been provided. One of the most effective ways to manage follow-ups is by utilizing a Customer Relationship Management (CRM) system.

A CRM system allows you to keep track of client information, interactions, and communication history in a centralized location, making it easier to plan and execute follow-ups. By leveraging the capabilities of a CRM, you can maximize efficiency and ensure that no client falls through the cracks. Here are some tips to help you get the most out of your CRM:

Keep client information up-to-date: Regularly update your CRM with accurate and current information about your clients. This includes contact details, preferences, and any significant life events that may have occurred since your last interaction. Accurate information will enable you to tailor your follow-up communication to be more personalized and relevant.

Set reminders and tasks: Use the CRM's built-in reminder and task features to schedule follow-up calls, emails, or meetings. This will help you stay organized and ensure that you never miss an opportunity to touch base with a client.

Segment your client list: Categorize your clients based on their needs, preferences, or stage in the grieving process. By segmenting your client list, you can create targeted follow-up campaigns that address the specific needs and concerns of each group.

Track your interactions: Record every interaction you have with your clients, including phone calls, emails, and meetings. This will give you a clear understanding of the history of your relationship and allow you to identify any areas that may require further attention or follow-up.

Log good impression data: Was there a dog barking in the background on your last call? Log it. Did a client cancel an appointment because they had kidney stones? Log it. Was your call cut short because your client was on vacation in Barbados? Log it. The more details you have, the easier it will be for you to build rapport on future calls.

————

During my time in the cosmetics industry, I frequently participated in women's expos. My booth was designed with a thoughtful setup: a table displaying products, a raffle basket, and hundreds of raffle cards. Positioned behind me, out of reach for event attendees, was the container where completed raffle cards were collected for the drawing. This strategic arrangement served a purpose.

My intention was to have attendees hand their raffle cards directly to me, allowing me to place them in the container. In the brief moments between receiving the card and placing it into the container, I would jot down quick, memorable details about the potential client on the card. This tactic helped me make a lasting impression during follow-up calls.

For instance, if I noted down "baby with curly hair eating a lollipop" on a card, I could begin my conversation by asking, "Did that lollipop get stuck in those beautiful curls?" This approach immediately conveyed to the prospective client that they were more than just a raffle card to me – they were a person I genuinely remembered and cared about.

Monitor and measure success: Regularly review the effectiveness of your follow-up efforts. Look for patterns and trends in your CRM data to identify areas where you may need to adjust your approach or communication style.

By utilizing a CRM system and implementing these tips, you can ensure consistent and meaningful follow-ups with your clients. This will help you maintain long-term relationships and demonstrate your commitment to providing ongoing support and care to the families you serve.

PROVIDE ONGOING SUPPORT

One of the most effective ways to foster long-term relationships with your clients is by offering ongoing support even after the initial sale. In deathcare, this means being available to address their concerns, answer questions, and provide guidance throughout the various stages of their journey. By maintaining a helpful and supportive presence, you'll demonstrate your genuine care for their well-being, leading to stronger connections and higher client satisfaction.

Regular Check-ins: Implement scheduled check-ins with your clients to ensure their well-being and offer any necessary assistance. These check-ins can be conducted through various channels such as phone calls, emails, or even in-person visits. For families who have already completed their advanced planning, I recommend a 90-day check-in. Every 90 days, reach out to them using different methods.

One contact could be a postcard, followed by a phone call, and then an email. The objective is to demonstrate to your clients that you are thinking of them and remain committed to providing ongoing support. This consistent outreach helps strengthen the relationship and reassures them of your continued dedication to their needs.

Offer Grief Resources: Be proactive in sharing grief resources, such as support groups, counseling services, and educational materials. Your clients may not always know where to turn for help; by providing them with relevant information, you'll make their journey a little easier.

Be Responsive: Respond promptly to any inquiries or concerns your clients may have. Whether it's a question about their end-of-life arrangements or a request for additional support, being attentive and responsive will show your clients that you're invested in their well-being.

Seek Feedback: Regularly ask for feedback from your clients to learn how you can better serve them. Their insights can help you identify areas for improvement and tailor your support to their unique needs.

Celebrate Milestones and Anniversaries: Recognize important dates, such as the anniversary of a loved one's passing, by sending a thoughtful message or card. This small gesture can mean a lot to grieving families and demonstrates your ongoing commitment to their emotional well-being. It can be as simple as having a recurring reminder in your CRM.

By providing ongoing support, you'll strengthen your relationships with existing clients and increase the likelihood of referrals and repeat business. In the deathcare industry, where trust and empathy are paramount, your commitment to your clients' well-being will make a lasting impact and contribute to your long-term success.

REFERRALS AND TESTIMONIALS

Building strong relationships with your clients often leads to referrals and testimonials, which can be instrumental in growing your business. By fostering long-term relationships and providing exceptional service, you increase the likelihood of clients recommending your services to their friends and family.

When facing a shortage of potential clients for advanced planning discussions, referrals can be the solution. By efficiently obtaining referrals from each family you assist with advanced planning, you can ensure a continuous supply of leads and maintain a thriving business.

When seeking referrals, follow the "Fight Club" rule: <u>Avoid using the word "referral" itself.</u> This term shifts the focus onto you rather than the support and service you've provided. Instead, concentrate on discussing the ways you have helped and served your clients, and express your eagerness to extend that same level of care to others. This approach maintains a client-centered conversation, emphasizing your commitment to providing valuable assistance to those in need.

Numerous strategies exist for acquiring referrals, but let's concentrate on just two. By mastering Method #1 and employing Method #2 when appropriate, you can effectively double your business within the next year through your dedicated efforts.

REFERRAL GENERATION METHOD #1

When you are finishing up an appointment with a client, ask for referrals. If they're pleased with your service, they'll be more than happy to share their experience with others. I use a 2-step process to generate referrals from advanced planning clients.

1. Affirm the positive experience. Injecting a little humor, I usually say something like, "Well, we try not to make the advanced planning process hurt too badly…" This usually results in a family replying with "No, that didn't hurt at all!" or "You made it much more pleasant than we expected it to be."

2. Upon receiving their positive feedback, seize the opportunity to inquire about others who might benefit from your services. You might say, "I'm delighted to hear that! My goal is to ensure everyone I meet with obtains the necessary information to make well-informed decisions for their families. Speaking of families, who's the first person who comes to mind who would also appreciate the valuable information you received today?" By requesting just one referral, you simplify the task for your client, freeing them from mentally scanning their entire contact list. Consequently, they are more likely to share the first person who comes to mind, fostering a smooth and effective referral process.

REFERRAL GENERATION METHOD #2

Use this method if you're currently frustrated with a lack of leads. Focus on families who have laid a loved one to rest with your assistance within the last 1 to 5 years, and leverage the education, information, or free resources you provided them. These families have firsthand experience with the benefits of your services and can be a valuable source of referrals.

1. Reach out and follow up. Initiate contact with families who have utilized your services in the past, expressing your condolences and checking in on their well-being. This genuine concern can help reestablish rapport and trust.

2. Highlight the resources provided. Remind them of the education, information, or free resources you shared during their experience with you. Reinforce the value these resources offered and how they contributed to a smoother process during their time of need.

3. Actively inquire about potential referrals. Once they've expressed satisfaction with your services and resources, confidently ask for referrals. You could say, "I'm glad to know that our services and resources were helpful to you during that difficult time. Who's the first person who comes to mind who could also benefit from the support, guidance, and valuable resources we provided?"

4. Offer gratitude and maintain communication: Thank your clients for any referrals they provide, and assure them that you'll handle their contacts with the same level of care and professionalism that you displayed to them. Keep them updated on any positive outcomes resulting from the referrals, and maintain an ongoing relationship with them to foster future referral opportunities.

By actively focusing on families who have already experienced the value of your services and resources, you can generate referrals from a group that truly understands and appreciates the importance of advanced planning and the support you provide.

Gather Testimonials: Testimonials play a crucial role in providing social proof and validating the quality of your services. When potential clients come across positive reviews from satisfied customers, it builds trust and confidence in your ability to meet their needs. After delivering excellent service, it is valuable to ask your clients if they would be open to sharing their experience through a written or video testimonial. To make it convenient for them, you can offer a straightforward testimonial form or provide guidelines on what they could include in their review. This approach encourages clients to provide feedback and helps you collect compelling testimonials that can be used to showcase your expertise and reassure potential clients of the quality of your services.

Share Success Stories: Sharing success stories on your website and social media channels is a powerful way to showcase the impact of your services. By highlighting the positive experiences of your clients, you can demonstrate your expertise and the value you bring to families during their time of need. Success stories also humanize your business and create an emotional connection with potential clients.

Maintain a Strong Online Presence: Encourage your clients to leave reviews on platforms like Google, Yelp, and Facebook. A strong online presence with positive reviews can significantly impact your business growth. If you're not the business owner, ask your clients to mention you by name in their review. Monitor these platforms regularly, respond to reviews (both positive and negative), and address any concerns to demonstrate your commitment to customer satisfaction.

Referrals and testimonials are crucial components of business growth in the deathcare industry. By cultivating strong relationships with your clients and encouraging them to share their positive experiences, you can build a solid reputation and attract new clients who trust and value your services.

Fostering long-term relationships in the deathcare industry is vital for both your professional success and the well-being of the families you serve. By turning complaints into sales opportunities, consistently following up with clients, providing ongoing support, and gathering referrals and testimonials, you can create a strong network of satisfied clients who become advocates for your services.

Building these lasting relationships not only helps your business grow but it also demonstrates your genuine care and commitment to the families you serve during their time of need. By focusing on nurturing long-term connections, you will establish yourself as a trusted and valued partner in the deathcare industry, ultimately making a profound difference in the lives of those you serve.

CHAPTER 11
EXCELLING AS A SALES LEADER

"HIRE SLOW AND FIRE FAST." These powerful words have resonated with me ever since I first encountered them at a management conference nearly twenty years ago. In the context of the deathcare industry, where sensitivity and emotion often influence our decisions as sales leaders, these words hold even greater significance.

It can be tempting to hold on to non-performing sales professionals due to the nature of our work. The truth remains, though, that retaining individuals who fail to regularly contribute to the team's goals only brings down the overall performance and sets a detrimental example for others.

When our efforts in performance management prove ineffective, it is crucial to liberate ourselves from salespeople who are not meeting expectations and, in turn, offer them the opportunity to find a position that aligns better with their strengths.

On the contrary, adopting a slow hiring approach allows us to thoroughly assess candidates and verify that they possess the necessary skills, qualities, and alignment with our organization's values.

By investing adequate time and effort into the selection process, we increase the likelihood of finding individuals who are not only capable but also deeply passionate about the work we do.

The aim of hiring slowly is not to unnecessarily prolong the recruitment process, but rather to ensure that each new team member is chosen with careful consideration. By taking the time to select individuals who possess the right combination of skills, values, and passion, you are establishing a solid foundation for a high-performing team that is dedicated to delivering exceptional service to your clients.

By embracing the principle of hiring slow and firing fast, we prioritize the success of our team as a whole. This approach allows us to maintain a high-performance culture where every member is motivated, engaged, and accountable for their contributions. It also sends a clear message to the rest of the team that subpar performance is not tolerated, fostering an environment of excellence and continuous improvement.

Remember, our goal as sales leaders is to cultivate a team of dedicated and high-achieving professionals who are passionate about delivering exceptional service to the families we serve. This means making difficult decisions when necessary and freeing ourselves and others from positions that are not the right fit. By doing so, we create opportunities for growth, elevate our team's performance, and ultimately ensure the success of our organization in the deathcare industry.

In this chapter, we will explore practical strategies and actionable tips for hiring the right people, training and developing your team, motivating and recognizing their efforts, and establishing a culture that embodies the most important aspects of the deathcare industry – empathy and service.

HIRING THE RIGHT PEOPLE

When aiming to build a high-performing team, look for the right balance between skills and innate characteristics in each prospective team member. While certain skills, such as sales techniques, can be taught and developed through training, innate characteristics like compassion and empathy cannot be easily cultivated. Therefore, you must prioritize these natural traits when hiring new team members.

1. Prioritize innate characteristics: During the hiring process, place a strong emphasis on identifying candidates who demonstrate genuine compassion, empathy, and emotional intelligence. These innate traits are vital in the deathcare industry, as they enable your team members to connect with and support grieving families in an authentic and meaningful way. While skills can be developed over time, innate characteristics are much harder to change or teach.

2. Assess soft skills: In addition to evaluating a candidate's technical skills and qualifications, pay close attention to their soft skills, such as active listening, communication, and problem-solving abilities. These skills can be harder to teach than technical skills.

3. Focus on potential: When assessing candidates, consider their potential for growth and development within your organization. While they may not possess all the necessary skills at the time of hiring, individuals with strong innate characteristics and a willingness to learn can be trained to become highly effective team members.

4. Evaluate willingness to put in the work: Sales roles require a proactive mindset and strong work ethic. Assess candidates' willingness to go beyond the typical clock-punching mentality by evaluating their commitment to prospecting, networking, and growing their contact list. Ask questions during the interview process that gauge their initiative, drive, and motivation to excel in a sales role. For example, you can inquire about their previous experiences in overcoming challenges, their approach to building professional networks, or their strategies for reaching new clients.

By carefully selecting the right individuals to join your team, you'll lay the foundation for a high-performing, cohesive group that is well-equipped to provide exceptional service and support to the families you serve.

TRAINING AND DEVELOPMENT

Once you have assembled a team of compassionate and proactive individuals, it's time to invest in their training and development to ensure they reach their full potential. A comprehensive and ongoing training program will enhance their skills but and boost their confidence, ultimately leading to improved performance and higher job satisfaction.

Orientation and onboarding: Begin by providing a thorough orientation and onboarding process for new hires. Include an overview of your organization's mission, values, and goals, as well as a detailed introduction to the products and services you offer. Ensure that new team members are familiar with the company culture, internal processes, and expectations for their roles.

Product knowledge: In-depth knowledge of your products and services is essential for any sales professional. Provide regular training sessions and updates on new offerings or changes to existing products. Encourage team members to ask questions and seek clarification on any aspects about which they are uncertain, fostering an environment of continuous learning and growth.

Sales skills: While some team members may have a natural aptitude for sales, refining and developing these skills is vital to their success. Provide training on various sales techniques, such as building rapport, identifying client needs, overcoming objections, and closing deals. Incorporate role-playing exercises and real-life scenarios to help your team members practice and apply these skills in a safe and supportive environment.

Emotional intelligence: As the deathcare industry involves dealing with clients who are going through a difficult and emotional time, it is crucial to develop your team's emotional intelligence. This includes providing training on empathy, active listening, effective communication, and managing their own emotions. It is important to help your team members understand the significance of being emotionally attuned to clients and offer strategies for building strong connections with them based on trust and understanding.

By prioritizing the training and development of your team members, you will equip them with the necessary skills and knowledge to excel in their roles while also demonstrating your commitment to their personal and professional growth. This investment in their development will lead to a more skilled, confident, and motivated team, ultimately contributing to the success of your organization in the deathcare industry.

MOTIVATION AND RECOGNITION

A motivated and engaged team is key to organization success, particularly in the deathcare industry, where empathy and compassion are vital components of exceptional service. To foster a high-performing team, focus on motivation and recognition, ensuring that your team members feel valued, appreciated, and inspired to continually improve.

Set clear goals and expectations: Clearly communicate the goals and expectations for your team, both individually and collectively. Establishing a shared vision and a sense of purpose will help motivate your team members to strive for excellence in their roles. Regularly review progress towards these goals and adjust them as needed to keep your team focused and engaged.

Provide autonomy and opportunities for growth: Empower your team members by giving them the autonomy to make decisions and take ownership of their work. Offer opportunities for growth and development, such as challenging projects, cross-training, or leadership roles. By trusting and investing in your team, you'll foster a sense of pride in their work and inspire them to set lofty goals for themselves, then work to achieve them.

Recognize and celebrate achievements: Acknowledge and celebrate your team members' accomplishments, both large and small. Recognition can take many forms, such as verbal praise, awards, bonuses, and team celebrations. By showing appreciation for their hard work and dedication, you'll boost morale and encourage continued effort and success.

Provide regular feedback: Offer consistent and constructive feedback to help your team members grow and improve in their roles. Establish a two-way dialogue, encouraging them to share their thoughts, concerns, and ideas. By maintaining open lines of communication, you'll build trust and rapport, which can contribute significantly to motivation and engagement.

By focusing on motivation and recognition, you'll create an environment where your team members feel valued, engaged, and inspired to excel in their roles. This will lead to improved performance, increased job satisfaction, and a more successful organization in the deathcare industry.

CULTIVATING A CULTURE OF EMPATHY AND SERVICE

The real question isn't "Do I affect my team's culture?" but rather, "How do I affect my team's culture?" You have a key role in forming the atmosphere that your team encounters every day. Building a service-focused culture makes a setting where team members feel confident in giving the best support possible to the families they serve. Let's look at some important ways to build this kind of culture:

1. Lead by example. Set the tone for your team by embodying service in everything you do. Leading by example demonstrates your commitment and inspires your team members to adopt the same mindset and approach.

———

Imagine being at a busy chain coffee shop when the regional manager is visiting. You can usually tell because the staff seem more tense and quiet. Recently, while I was enjoying my pumpkin spice latte with coconut milk and working on an article about cremation permanent placement, I noticed the regional manager sitting nearby, observing an overwhelmed team trying to serve a growing line of customers. He just sat there, making notes on his notepad.

The message he was sending to his employees was clear: he considered himself too important to jump in and help serve customers. The growing line of customers became increasingly agitated. The situation could have easily been alleviated if the manager had stepped in to make a few lattes. By doing so, he would have gained the respect and gratitude of his team.

Unfortunately, as people climb the corporate ladder, they often distance themselves from the most important work in the company - the customer-facing work. As a sales leader, I firmly believe in never asking my team to do anything I wouldn't be willing to do myself when needed. This includes prospecting, meeting with families, making copies, or vacuuming the office. Leading by example is crucial to fostering a culture of empathy and service, and to helping you avoid becoming a manager who considers yourself too important for certain work.

2. Practice active listening. Make a conscious effort to listen attentively and understand your team members' concerns, ideas, and emotions. Demonstrate care and interest in their well-being, encouraging them to do the same when working with clients and colleagues.

I'll always remember the first family I served as they laid their infant to rest. The experience of a baby burial is unforgettable. It stays with you. However, the most haunting burial I ever conducted was when my son Ryan was 17 years old. It involved a girl of the same age who had taken her own life. The process of meeting her parents and attending the service was incredibly taxing.

A moment at the end of the service is forever etched in my memory. The grieving mother stood at the foot of her daughter's casket, leaned over, and pressed her cheek against the wood. On her right side was her husband, the girl's father, gently rubbing her back. On her left was her college-aged son, who also tried to comfort her with a soothing touch. As the girl's father and brother attempted to console her with muffled sobs, she let out a heart-wrenching wail that echoed throughout the cemetery, and still echoes in my mind today.

———

The emotional effect of dealing with end-of-life situations on workers, especially when they're new to it, is very important. Think back to your own early experiences as you help and guide those new to the job. By making sure they have a safe space to reflect and relax when they need it, you can support their emotional health and ability to bounce back. Listen without judging or assuming. Reduce distractions and focus only on your team member who needs help. This allows you to offer resources like mentorship or counseling services. In the end, creating a caring environment will benefit your team and improve the level of kindness and understanding they give to the families they serve.

3. Be consistent in your actions. Consistency in your actions and behavior helps establish trust and credibility with your team members. Ensure that you consistently uphold the values of empathy and service, even when faced with difficult decisions or challenging circumstances.

When you lead by example and consistently embody the values of empathy and service, you can inspire your team to adopt a similar mindset and approach in their work. This, in turn, will create a culture where team members feel supported, engaged, and motivated to provide the best possible care and service to the families they serve.

BUILDING A SUPPORTIVE TEAM ENVIRONMENT

Creating a supportive team environment is essential for fostering empathy and providing exceptional service. Here are additional tips to build a supportive team environment:

1. Encourage collaboration. Foster a collaborative team environment where team members can share ideas, support one another, and work together to overcome challenges. Encourage cross-functional collaboration and provide opportunities for team members to learn from each other's experiences.

2. Promote work-life balance. Recognize the importance of work-life balance and support your team members in maintaining a healthy equilibrium. Encourage them to take breaks, use their vacation time, and engage in activities that help them recharge and maintain their well-being.

3. Provide resources and support. Ensure that your team members have access to resources and support to help them navigate the emotional challenges of the deathcare industry. This can include providing counseling services, mentorship programs, or peer support networks.

4. Foster a learning culture. Create a culture of continuous learning and improvement by encouraging ongoing education and professional development. Support team members in pursuing relevant certifications, attending industry conferences, or participating in training programs that enhance their skills and knowledge.

5. Celebrate diversity and inclusivity. Embrace diversity and create an inclusive environment where every team member feels respected and valued. Promote diversity in hiring practices and ensure equal opportunities for growth and advancement within the organization.

By combining the elements of building and leading a high-performing team with cultivating a culture of service, you'll create a dynamic and supportive environment where your team members thrive, and your clients receive the compassionate care and guidance they deserve. Remember, as a leader, your commitment to building a dynamic team will contribute to the overall success and fulfillment of everyone involved, including your clients, in this emotionally-charged industry.

CHAPTER 12
STRATEGIES FOR CONTINUOUS IMPROVEMENT

IN THE DYNAMIC and ever-evolving deathcare industry, the key to long-term success lies in a commitment to continuous improvement. By consistently assessing and refining your strategies and practices, you ensure that your team stays ahead of the curve, adapts to changing market conditions, and continues to deliver exceptional service to the families you serve.

This chapter will look into some key ways to build a culture of ongoing improvement. We'll discuss the value of monitoring and studying performance, learning from both failures and victories, and adjusting to industry changes. By using these strategies in your leadership style, you'll inspire your team to learn, come up with new ideas, and excel in their roles, ultimately leading to long-term success.

PERFORMANCE TRACKING AND ANALYSIS

Louis V. Gerstner, Jr. said, "People don't do what you expect but what you inspect." Success happens in the day-to-day, hour-to-hour, and minute-to-minute activities. While some aspects of sales performance are beyond our control, we can, and must, focus on the factors that we can influence. By tracking and sharing behavioral key performance indicators (KPIs), you can create a culture of accountability, empowerment, and continuous improvement within your team.

Behavioral KPIs are metrics that measure specific actions taken by your team members, which can have a direct impact on their overall performance. Here are some examples of behavioral KPIs that can be tracked and shared within your organization:

1. Number of outreach calls made: Tracking the number of calls made by your team members helps to ensure that they are actively reaching out to potential clients and staying engaged with existing customers.

2. Number of hours spent actively networking: Networking is an essential component of business development in the deathcare industry. By monitoring the time spent on networking activities, you can encourage your team members to build and maintain strong relationships within the community.

3. Number of appointments set: Setting appointments is a key step in the sales process, as it allows your team to showcase your services and engage with potential clients. Tracking the number of appointments set can help you identify areas for improvement in your team's outreach efforts.

4. **Number of new leads added into CRM:** Without adding new prospects into your Customer Relationship Manager, your team will simply be calling the same people over and over. Generating new leads through referrals, networking, file diving, and prospecting is crucial to growth.

To make the most of these behavioral KPIs, consider the following:

Set clear expectations: Establish guidelines and targets for each behavioral KPI to ensure your team members understand what is expected of them and how their performance will be measured.

Regularly monitor and analyze performance data: Collect and review data on your team's behavioral KPIs consistently to identify trends, areas for improvement, and best practices.

Share insights and provide feedback: Communicate the results of your performance analysis with your team members. Highlight their achievements while providing constructive feedback on areas that need improvement.

Develop action plans for improvement: Based on your analysis, create specific action plans to address any performance gaps. This may involve providing additional training, refining processes, or setting new goals for your team members.

Continuously review and adjust: Periodically revisit your behavioral KPIs to ensure they remain relevant and aligned with your organization's objectives. Adjust targets and expectations as needed to maintain a focus on continuous improvement.

By inspecting what you expect, behavioral KPIs, you can empower your team to take control of their performance and contribute to the overall success of your organization. For a few industry-specific tracking templates and resources, visit sellingwithsensitivity.com/bonuses.

EMBRACING FEEDBACK

Your journey to mastering empathy and service is an ongoing process. It is crucial to continuously grow and learn to ensure that you remain effective, compassionate, and well-prepared to support grieving families. Feedback is one of the most valuable sources of learning, and it can come from clients, colleagues, and even from ourselves. Embracing feedback is essential for our personal and professional development. Here are some strategies to welcome and make the most of feedback to enhance your career growth:

Foster a Feedback-friendly Environment: Create a safe and open atmosphere where families, colleagues, and employees feel comfortable sharing their feedback and experiences. Encourage honest and constructive communication and emphasize the importance of learning from both positive and negative feedback.

Actively Seek Feedback: Proactively request feedback from clients, team members, and industry peers. This may involve asking for reviews, conducting surveys, or initiating conversations about your services and performance. By actively seeking feedback, you demonstrate your commitment to improvement and growth.

Listen with an Open Mind: Accept feedback with an open mind and a readiness to learn. Avoid the temptation to get defensive or ignore what's being said; instead, listen closely to the concerns or ideas being shared. Think about how the feedback connects to your job and what changes you can make to better serve your community.

Identify Areas for Improvement: Use the feedback you receive to pinpoint specific areas where you can improve your skills, knowledge, or services. This may involve enhancing your communication techniques, expanding your understanding of cultural differences in grief, or refining your approach to tailoring services to individual needs.

Implement Changes: Take proactive steps to implement the changes or improvements suggested by the feedback you receive. This could involve updating policies, investing in training programs, modifying your service offerings, or simply by tweaking your behaviors. By putting feedback into action, you showcase your commitment to continuous improvement and your dedication to providing compassionate, high-quality care. This not only benefits your clients but also strengthens your professional reputation.

Monitor Progress: Regularly evaluate your progress in response to the feedback you've received. Assess whether the changes you've made have led to improvements in your services, client satisfaction, or personal growth. Use this information to guide your future development and to refine your approach as needed.

Recognize and Celebrate Growth: Acknowledge and celebrate the progress you make because of embracing feedback. Recognize the value of feedback in shaping your personal and professional growth, and express gratitude to those who have contributed to your development.

By embracing feedback, you create opportunities for growth and learning that will enhance your ability to provide compassionate, empathetic, and effective support to grieving families. Continual growth and learning are essential for all deathcare professionals, ensuring that we continually adapt and evolve in our mission to serve with empathy and understanding.

PURSUING PROFESSIONAL DEVELOPMENT OPPORTUNITIES

In addition to embracing feedback, actively pursuing professional development opportunities is a great way to continuously grow and improve in the deathcare industry. By seeking out new experiences, knowledge, and skills, you can ensure that you stay up-to-date, well-equipped, and adaptable in your profession. Here are some strategies to consider when pursuing professional development opportunities:

Attend Industry Conferences and Workshops: Regularly participate in conferences, workshops, and seminars specific to the deathcare industry. These events offer invaluable opportunities to learn from experts, stay current on industry trends, and network with other professionals who share your passion for compassionate service.

Enroll in Continuing Education Courses: Seek out courses and certifications that can enhance your skills and knowledge in areas such as grief counseling, cultural competency, or funeral planning. Continuing education not only enriches your professional capabilities but also demonstrates your commitment to staying informed and maintaining a high level of expertise.

Join Professional Organizations: Become a member of professional associations related to the deathcare industry, such as the National Funeral Directors Association, the Cremation Association of North America, and the International Cemetery, Cremation and Funeral Association. Membership in these organizations provides access to valuable resources, networking opportunities, and industry-specific education.

Network with Industry Peers: Cultivate relationships with colleagues and other professionals in your field, both locally and nationally. Networking can provide opportunities for mentorship, collaboration, and the exchange of ideas and best practices, all of which contribute to your professional growth.

Stay Informed on Industry News: Regularly read industry publications, blogs, and news articles to stay informed about changes, trends, and innovations in the deathcare sector. Staying up-to-date on the latest developments will help you adapt and evolve in your profession.

Engage in Self-Reflection and Self-Assessment: Take the time to reflect on your own performance, skills, and knowledge. Identify areas where you feel confident and areas where you could benefit from further development. This self-assessment can help you prioritize and target your professional development efforts more effectively.

Set Professional Goals: Establish clear and achievable goals for your professional growth, such as obtaining a specific certification, improving your communication skills, or expanding your understanding of a particular area of grief support. Having concrete goals can help you stay focused and motivated in your pursuit of professional development.

Embrace Lifelong Learning: Cultivate a mindset of lifelong learning and continuous improvement. View every experience, interaction, and challenge as an opportunity to learn and grow, both personally and professionally.

By actively pursuing professional development opportunities, you demonstrate your commitment to excellence and your dedication to providing the highest level of service and support to grieving families. As you continue to grow and evolve in your profession, you will become an even more

compassionate, empathetic, and effective deathcare professional, capable of making a lasting impact in the lives of those
you serve.

Continuous improvement is crucial to maintaining
competitiveness and achieving success in the deathcare
industry. By implementing strategies such as performance
tracking and analysis, learning from setbacks and successes,
and adapting to industry changes, you can ensure that your
team is consistently evolving and growing. Foster a culture
that encourages open communication, personal growth, and
resilience. This will position your sales organization to navigate future challenges and seize opportunities. Remember,
the pursuit of excellence is an ongoing journey. Your willingness to learn and adapt will distinguish your team and pave
the way for long-term success.

CHAPTER 13
CONCLUSION

MY DAD WAS *an incredible piano player. Though he never received formal training and couldn't read sheet music, he played by ear, having learned to play as a boy by observing his brother's fingers during classical lessons. I grew up regularly observing my dad listen to a piece of music, pause it, try it, rewind it, listen again, and try again. This cycle continued until he mastered the song and added it to his vast repertoire, eventually amassing thousands of songs in several large binders. Dad enjoyed a 45-year career doing what he loved—entertaining. The baby grand piano he played for more than three decades now resides in my living room. Sometimes, as I stand beside it and close my eyes, I can almost hear my dad's distinctive version of "Moonlight Sonata."*

At the time of this book's publishing, my dad has been gone for more than eight years.

Healing unfolds so gradually and subtly that it's almost imperceptible. Now, when I talk about my dad, I can genuinely smile, no longer fearing that just the mention of his name will trigger uncontrolled sobs or force me to smile through my tears.

Assisting families, either directly or through a team member, in planning their end-of-life arrangements has become a source of healing for me. With each opportunity to offer support, I feel more healed because I understand all too well the pain they are sparing their loved ones—a pain that I have personally endured.

Unanswered questions linger in the recesses of my mind. Did I make the choices he would have wanted? Should I have done something differently?

I suspect that I'll carry these questions with me for the rest of my life.

The ache of missing my dad never entirely dissipates. I will always miss him, and this gives me a unique perspective when serving families—a perspective that cannot be bought or taught.

It's clear that deathcare sales transcends being just a job or career—it's a vocation that offers a rare opportunity to leave a lasting impact on the families we serve. The rewards of a career in this industry are both personal and professional, as we play an essential role in helping families confront and plan for their own mortality, protect their loved ones, and navigate their grief, all while achieving success and financial stability.

Working in deathcare brings numerous benefits. It ensures job security since people will always require assistance in laying their loved ones to rest and making end-of-life arrangements. Moreover, it allows us to make a meaningful difference in the lives of others.

There is no shame in selling deathcare products and services. Embrace the privilege that comes with choosing deathcare as your sales focus, and build a prosperous career while providing comfort and solace to families instead of pressuring them into unnecessary purchases that will eventually lose their value and significance.

Your work in deathcare sales empowers you to make a profound difference in the lives of those you serve, guiding them through their darkest moments and enabling them to make informed decisions that align with their unique needs and desires. By prioritizing your clients' well-being and approaching each interaction with genuine care and concern, you can create an enduring impact that transcends the transactional nature of sales.

I challenge you to take immediate action. Lean into empathy, connection, and authenticity in your work. Commit to delivering exceptional service that prioritizes the needs and desires of each family, approaching every interaction with a dedication to fostering genuine connections and lasting relationships.

We can shape a better future for the deathcare industry and the families who rely on us for kindness, understanding, and assistance.

Let's offer connection, hope, healing, and support to families when they need it most, whether they're coping with loss or planning for the future.

Together, let's transcend the boundaries of tradition and leave the stigma behind. By challenging outdated norms and embracing compassion, empathy, and service, we have the power to create an industry that is compassionate, inclusive, and forward-thinking.

Let's approach our work with unwavering dedication, determined to build a future for deathcare that exceeds expectations, breaks barriers, and brings solace to those who need it most.

The time is now to take the lead.

The future of deathcare rests in our capable hands, and it is us, together, who will shape the industry that leaves the stigma behind.

To access the *Selling with Sensitivity* bonus material, visit
sellingwithsensitivity.com/bonuses

ACKNOWLEDGMENTS

First I want to express my heartfelt gratitude to Gloria Jabro, my mom, teacher, motivator, morning phone call, and built-in best friend. Your unwavering presence and support in my life is immeasurable.

A special thank you to my amazing wife, Sarah, for lending me your ear and always being willing to listen to the stories of my day, whether they're heartwarming or heartbreaking. You are my primary source of emotional support, uncontrollable laughter, and clean laundry. I love life with you.

I'm deeply grateful to Ken Wachsberger, Kimberly Jacobs, and Heather Oberlin for the invaluable contributions in enhancing the flow, clarity, and overall editing of this book. Your expertise has been instrumental in shaping the final result.

To my son, Ryan. From the moment I learned of your existence, you have inspired me to reach higher. I am immensely grateful for the lessons you have taught me, which I am certain outweigh the ones I have taught you. Being your mom fills me with pride and joy.

Lastly, I want to extend my appreciation to the clients and team members who have played a part in the stories and lessons shared in this book. I have changed the names mentioned in the book to ensure confidentiality and respect your privacy. Thank you for trusting me and for being an integral part of my journey.

ABOUT THE AUTHOR

Liza Altenburg is a passionate advocate for the "as if it were my own family" mentality in the deathcare industry. With over two decades experience in service-focused sales, Liza has honed her skills in understanding the unique needs and emotions of families who are confronting mortality.

A John Maxwell-certified trainer, speaker, and DISC behavior consultant, Liza brings a wealth of leadership expertise and motivational insights to her work. She helps professionals to understand and leverage their unique behavioral styles for greater success.

Liza continuously seeks opportunities to connect with fellow deathcare professionals. You can find her on LinkedIn (linkedin.com/in/lizaaltenburg), where she shares valuable insights, resources, and engaging discussions. You can also find her blog at lizaaltenburg.com.

A lifelong Metro Detroiter, Liza resides with her wife Sarah, son Ryan, and two dogs, Marty and Lucy. She regularly dances in the kitchen and laughs too hard at terrible puns. In her spare time, she can be found near a campfire or a swimming pool.

Selling with Sensitivity is Liza's first book, reflecting her commitment to helping deathcare professionals thrive through empathy, service, and connection. With her expertise and heartfelt approach, Liza is making a profound impact on the industry and the lives of those she serves.